Life Achievement
in the 21st Century

Life Achievement in the 21st Century

T.C. Lea

VANTAGE PRESS
New York

FIRST EDITION

All rights reserved, including the right of
reproduction in whole or in part in any form.

Copyright © 2006 by T.C. Lea

Published by Vantage Press, Inc.
419 Park Ave. South, New York, NY 10016

Manufactured in the United States of America
ISBN: 0-533-15298-4

Library of Congress Catalog Card No.: 2005906797

0 9 8 7 6 5 4 3 2 1

Contents

Figures vii
Acknowledgments ix
Introduction—Life Factors xi

1. The Life Mountain 1
2. Three Types of Self 20
3. Mind Factors 34
4. Innate Data Banks 48
5. Knowledge 66
6. Happiness and Life Satisfaction 70
7. Stress 77
8. Social Factors 82
9. The Life Mountain and Reality 92
10. Life Achievement 98

Appendix A 113
Appendix B 117
Bibliography 119

Figures

1. Individual Life Achievement — xvi
2. Self Realization and Life Achievement — xvii
3. The Life Mountain — 4
4. Three Types of Self — 23
5. Five Types of Mind — 24
6. The Self — 25
7. Personality — 28
8. The Individual Mind — 37
9. Thought and Ideas — 38
10. Understanding, Memory, Imagination, Will — 41
11. Emotion and Reason — 42
12. Intuitive Mind Operation — 47
13. Data Bank Functions — 51
14. Lower, Higher, Essence Data Banks — 52
15. Intelligence Development on the Life Mountain — 62
16. Knowledge — 69
17. Happiness and Life Satisfaction — 73
18. Stress — 81
19. Social Factors — 85
20. Life Mountain and Reality — 95
21. Life Achievement — 101
22. Life Achievement Forms — 102

Acknowledgments

I should like to thank the 2,000 senior managers, from twenty countries, who contributed research data and experience as background data for this book.

I should also like to thank Jane Francis for her computerized profiling of the twenty-two figures in this book.

Introduction—Life Factors

1. Recorded experience over the last 5,000 years indicates that individuals have a deep seated urge to achieve their life aim, which they know exists but they are not certain what it is. Thus they are faced with the problem of finding the best way to something cloaked in the mists of uncertainty. The intensity of the feeling about this life aim, and the importance attached to finding it, varies with individuals. For some it can be very strong and controls their approach to life in society, while for others its existence has limited realization by the conscious mind, because of its inadequate state of development. Nevertheless, its effects can still cause feelings of frustration and dissatisfaction with life. This book sets out to show that this deep-seated life aim is in fact a very important unconscious drive in the human mind and that its understanding and realization by the conscious mind can provide the deep satisfaction that we search for all our lives. In addition, this deep-seated unconscious life aim can affect the intensity and content of the feeling of hope for a better life during the lifespan. The first requirement in understanding this life aim is to examine our present position and why we are in it.

2. In society today there are many who have no knowledge of the higher levels of life satisfaction potentially available, let alone the higher level still of deep satisfaction giving full life realization. This is because there is no record of either in their memory, thus the mind evaluation system

can never apply them in making decisions or even think about them. Thus the lower levels of life satisfaction are assumed to be the only ones available with these coming from a high standard of material living, crime prevention and sex. Thus politicians wanting to maintain or gain power concentrate on improving the standard of material living and crime prevention, while parents desire examination success for their children from the education system, in order for them to compete in a market economy. In turn, politicians use material living standards and crime prevention as their measure of success, while parents use examination grades achieved and university entrance as keys to higher potential material living standards for their children and possibly future ego enhancement for themselves.

3. While high material living standards, crime prevention and examination success are all essential factors in a market economy providing effective utilization of resources, it can so easily provide only a low level of life achievement and life satisfaction. However, there are many once their higher material living standards have been achieved, require higher levels of life achievement in order to find that life is stimulating and really enjoyable. The resulting tension at being unable to achieve such a level of life achievement is at the unconscious level but appears in the conscious mind as a feeling of frustration with present life. In turn, this is an important cause of many of the social problems today. Thus the requirement to be able to achieve the higher levels of life satisfaction that result in a deeper feeling of realization in life. But to be successful such an approach must be achieved with the support of the individuals concerned, it must also be within the resources available and not generate additional workloads causing stress. In turn, this requires knowledge of the factors involved by all concerned. Thus knowledge of those entities that provide

the material, intellectual and spiritual forms that provide life achievement. This requires knowledge of the three types of self as the surface self as conscious mind, the inner self as the unconscious mind and the deep self as spiritual, plus their inter-relationship and how they integrate with the innate data bank structure of the mind. In turn this involves the five types of mind as intuitive, higher rational, lower rational, lust realization and instinctive. It is also necessary to understand the three levels of satisfaction and how each level contributes to life achievement. These three levels are lower level satisfaction, higher level satisfaction and deep satisfaction. All these factors are shown in outline in Figure 1 and are covered in this book using the concept that all theoretical analysis should be supported whenever possible by scientific analysis of relevant empirical activity.

4. Nature includes the environment, political systems, social systems, religions, human intelligence and human development comprising individual and social development. Nature uses pleasure and happiness to motivate human development, thus individuals who set out to realize their potential over the lifespan can expect to have a higher life satisfaction than those who do not. In order to effect this development, individuals are born with their minds containing innate mental characteristics that are brought into activity during the lifespan. The use that the individual makes of these characteristics is termed self realization, which includes personality development in terms of the material, intellectual and spiritual. Thus self realization is individual activity that supports Nature's requirements and covers all relevant aspects of the individual's life activity. Self realization is closely connected with social development because the individual is never entirely free from the effects of the social in terms of thought, actions and resources. Life achievement at any particular time is the total

contribution self realization has made to meeting Nature's requirements since birth. In comparison life satisfaction refers to the feeling of the individual at any particular time in the lifespan. A summary of the factors affecting self realization and life achievement are given in Figure 2.

5. The definition of terms should be such that a common understanding can be achieved but this can prove difficult. For example, the self today can be defined as part of the Absolute in one particular group and yet in another group with a different philosophy and little religious influence, the self can be considered to be generated by the individual operating in society and the environment. Thus self realization in different groups can have different sets of defining factors. In order to reduce the problem of understanding of terms to a minimum the Life Mountain is used as an operating model to define, describe and integrate the relevant terms. In this respect the Life Mountain, as part of Nature, is based on the last 5,000 years of recorded experience and is applied in present situations using the material, intellectual and spiritual.

6. The Life Mountain is the entity on which individuals spend their lifespan in order to achieve life achievement in its various forms and includes mental and physical development. In terms of life achievement, knowledge requirements on the Life Mountain involve objective general principles and their application in particular situations. Objective general principles are required because the past 5,000 years of recorded experience indicates that a society without applying objective general principles, degenerates to the lowest subjective level consistent with material adequacy, with its associated low level intellectual activity. Thus the Life Mountain sets out to provide the best balance between objective general principles and their application in particular situations in an advanced market economy. In this con-

text experience has shown that individuals operating in their own areas of responsibility require objective general principles as guidelines, if rational self interest is to give adequate support to the family and society. In addition, adequate knowledge of relevant objective general principles when stored in memory can increase the effectiveness of decision making and help reduce stress.

7. Until the sixth century BCE knowledge was an integrated whole but since then it has been separated into subjects, due to the increased amount, depth and complexity of content. However, in the twenty-first century with its very rapid increase in scientific, technological and communication systems knowledge, it has become necessary to group eight subjects: psychology, mind, brain/body, sociology, theology, philosophy, metaphysics and high-energy physics. The inclusion of some aspects of high-energy physics is helpful in understanding of mind, brain and body operation. In order to obtain the best compromise of amount, width and depth of knowledge these eight subjects have been grouped into an integrated whole to provide objective general principles for use on the Life Mountain. This will enable individuals to be able to apply them as guidelines in their particular situations. This should reduce the time and effort spent on knowledge acquisition, thus enabling greater concentration of effort on dealing with practical solutions.

8. Background information for this book has come from recorded details of human development over the last 5,000 years. A list of the 184 chief thinkers who have been used is given in Appendix A, which also includes 27 religious aspects. The chief thinkers provided 60 philosophical aspects, 24 mind aspects and 9 high-energy physics aspects and these are given in Appendix B. Details of the 282 books used are given in the Bibliography. Additional background infor-

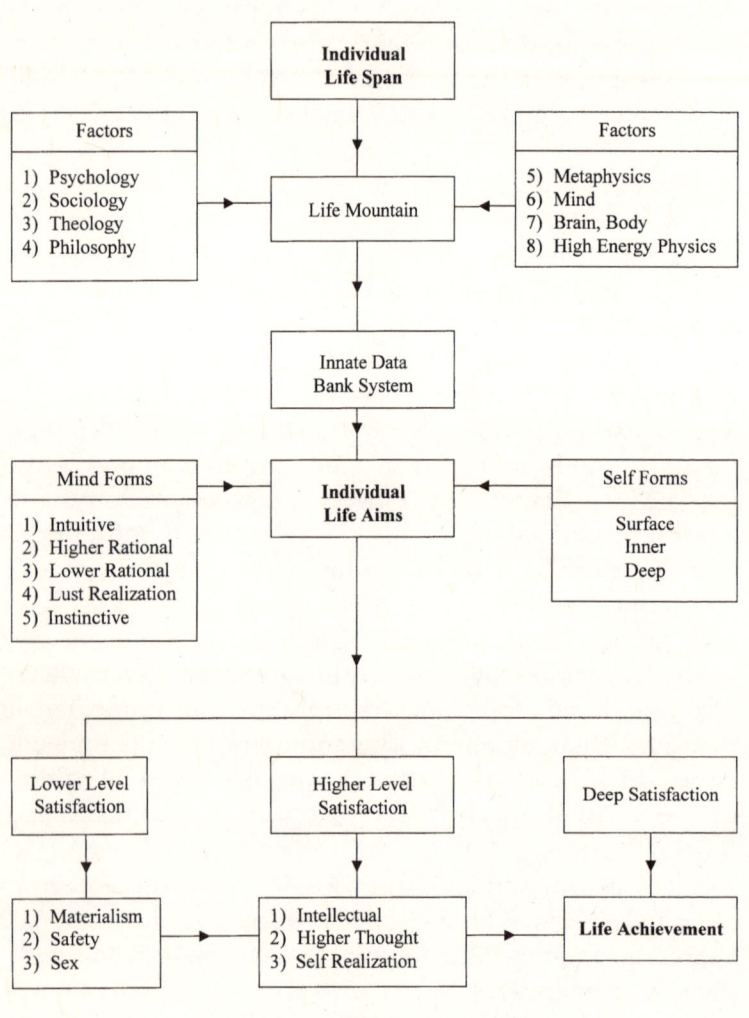

Figure 1
Individual Life Achievement

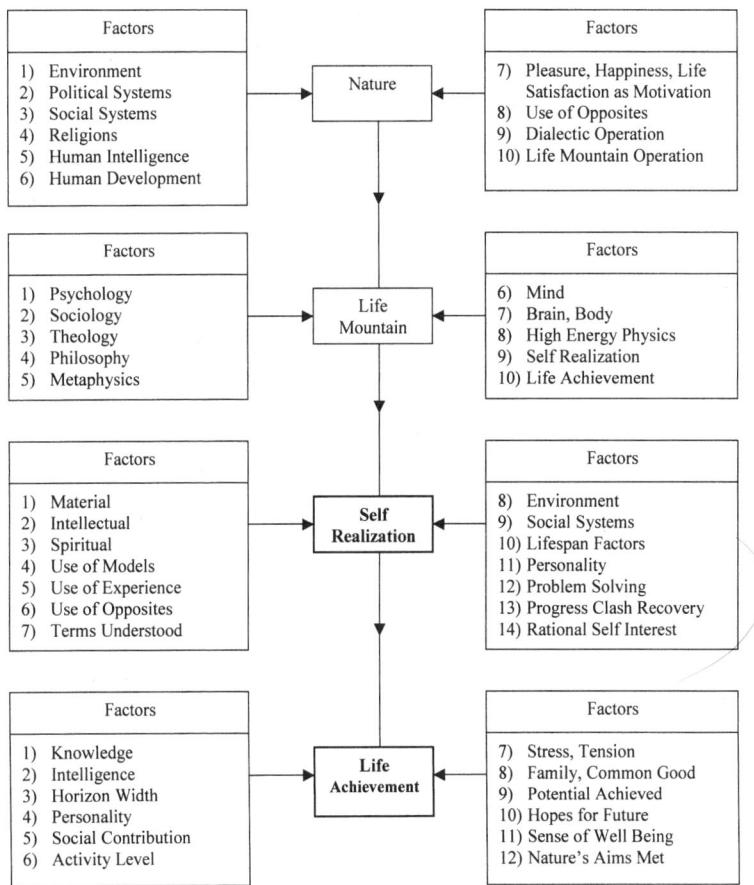

Figure 2: Self Realization and Life Achievement

mation has come from 140 five-day education management courses for 4,200 senior managers from 25 countries and from management short courses run for the Health Service, Social Services and Industry. Although run by Higher Education, all these short courses were run under strict market economy forces and generated an overall profit margin of 8 percent after all expenses, including salaries, had been met. During this program about 400 visits were made to State and Independent Schools in England, Wales and Scotland to discuss management projects implementation. These visits enabled a short analysis of the social aspects in the State school catchment areas to be made. This knowledge has been applied in Life Mountain analysis. Due to the confidential nature of the research data no details of individuals or institutions are given. The Life Mountain is covered in Chapter 1 and an outline is given in Figure 3.

Life Achievement in the 21st Century

1
The Life Mountain

1. The Life Mountain, as part of Nature, provides the actual situation for human collective intelligence to develop to perfection by time infinity. At the Creation, humanity was placed at the Base of the Life Mountain and provided with an innate unconscious drive to climb up the Life Mountain, by developing themselves and widening their horizons, from the minimum survival level at the Base, to eventually reaching perfection at time infinity. Nature also set the condition that individuals who maximize their contribution to this overall aim will also maximize their life satisfaction. Thus the maximization of life achievement during the lifespan will also maximize life satisfaction achievement over that period. Thus life satisfaction has a direct relation to human development in terms of the material, intellectual and spiritual. Lower level happiness is associated with the achievement of the material as safety, shelter, food, water, etc. Higher level happiness is associated with the intellectual as the aesthetic, deep feeling, deep emotion, the noble, the true, desire for improvement, will to succeed using higher level thought, etc. Deep satisfaction, from the deep self, is the highest form of conscious realization and is associated with the spiritual.

2. Individuals spend their lifespan on the Life Mountain in order to realize their mental and physical development in its various forms. In turn, this enables self

realization to take place with life achievement being the summation of self realization since birth. Thus self realization and life achievement are necessary for individuals to develop and make their contribution to the overall aim of Nature, as human perfection at the time infinity. In order for individuals to do this Nature provides three dimensions of life on the Life Mountain as the material, intellectual and spiritual. The superior dimension is the spiritual followed by the intellectual and material, with all three dimensions being essential for a fully realized individual life. Usually the spiritual is taken as contributing to the religious collective plus maintenance of ethical purity. Different environments, social systems, geographical situation, etc. express spirituality in different ways as the religions of the world and this includes dialectical materialism as the scientific form of religion. In addition, the individual can have spiritual feelings without belonging to a religion. However, the great advantage of religion is that it enables collective expression of the spiritual aspect but this does not negate the need for individual spirituality and this includes materialists and existentialists. The spiritual comes from the deep self via the intuitive mind and appears in the higher rational mind in conscious form.

3. The Summit of the Life Mountain sets the ultimate standard of human development as intellectual perfection, the widening of self-horizons to include all knowledge required to achieve perfect self realization, which also requires ethical perfection. The time is then infinity and all social systems will have merged into one perfect system, all innate data bank content in all individual minds will have achieved full development as complete perfection and all mind intelligent computers will have completed their development and the Life Mountain will be in a state of complete rest. At the Summit, the spirituality in individuals as

the deep self, by using the perfect intelligence reached as a foundation, will be able to comprehend the Absolute Spirit as the ultimate aim of all human life. At present, the Absolute Spirit is incomprehensible to humanity at its present stage of development. Perfection at the Summit sets the standard for assessment of present day levels of development and excellence.

4. In terms of the present time, the next level down from the Summit is the Potential Level that sets the standard to be reached by humanity operating with totally supporting circumstances, planning and implementation. At the Creation, the Potential Level was just above the Base and moved up the Life Mountain as humanity developed. In addition, humanity was provided with an innate urge to climb up to the Potential Level wherever it was located during their lifespan, by achieving self realization. But as well as being given this urge to climb up to the Potential Level humanity were also given free will not to, if they so desired. In addition, Nature also provided the feeling of pleasure, happiness and life satisfaction for those making the climb. The clash between the urge to climb up giving happiness, and free will not to, because of the extra effort required, is part of the polar dialectic operation of Nature on the Life Mountain, which is necessary to produce progress.

5. Human performance is not perfect and circumstances vary, so that the Actual Level reached on the Life Mountain will be lower than the Potential Level at any particular time. In terms of self realization the Actual Level reached by different individuals will vary due to circumstances, the use made of relevant experience, the use of free will, how Nature's motivating drives of pleasure, happiness and life satisfaction are used, innate data bank content, essence data bank content and genetic content. At birth each individual has an unconscious data bank content that is

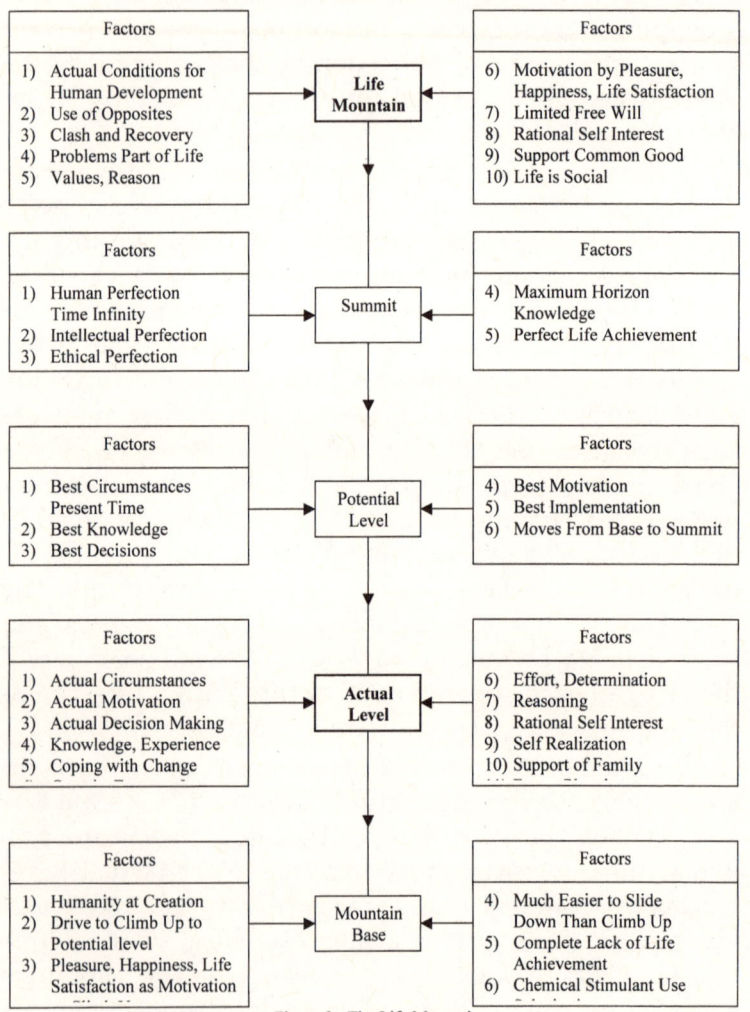

Figure 3: The Life Mountain

partly the same for all and partly varying for each individual. The data bank content is modulated by social conditioning during the lifespan and gives the unconscious drives into the conscious mind necessary for the individuals to climb up the Life Mountain, in terms of self realization. The essence data bank content is partly the same for all but has greater individual variation than the innate data bank content. The essence data bank content gives the mental development of the individual from birth to the end of the lifespan but is not modulated by social conditioning during the lifespan. The genetic content gives the physical development including the brain structure, with the genetic content coming from hereditary aspects. However, the genetic content activity level can be affected by the lack of body nourishment. There is also evidence that the genetic system can be modulated by the level of intensity of life factors affecting parents.

6. In terms of determinism, individuals are given no choice about being born or the level of society in which they are born but they have been given the potential to develop themselves and thus obtain a rewarding and satisfying life, as long as they meet Nature's requirements. These are to achieve self realization during the lifespan based on a rational self-interest, support of the family and contribution to the common good of society. In turn, for achieving these factors Nature provides a really satisfying life feeling. The individual will then be supporting the reason for being on the Life Mountain in the first place. However, there is no compulsion for the individual to follow all of Nature's requirements and within the free will allowed by Nature individuals can do otherwise. Thus individuals can follow lust drives instead of acting rationally, which is Nature's requirement. But if they do, in the longer term, they will lose happiness and life satisfaction because that is how Nature

operates. This can lead to a feeling of an unrealized life that can generate dissatisfaction. This occurs due to the changed circumstances brought about by the lust achievement. This follows because the Life Mountain has been created so that everything worthwhile in life has to be earned by rational effort not lust. Thus a satisfying life requires self realization that involves personality development involving ethical principles, supported by strength of character. In this respect it so much easier to slide down the Life Mountain to levels of increasing dissatisfaction with life in the longer term. Recorded experience over the last 5,000 years indicates that this is usually learnt the hard way.

7. Thus the need to estimate your potential and how to make the best use of it to the rational advantage of yourself, the family and the common good of society, because life on the Life Mountain is social. This requires the best use of personal relations and mutual support, with everything we do on the Life Mountain being affected by circumstances, surface values and unconscious drives, which can change. In addition, there is always the requirement for sufficient knowledge to make the best use of individual and social factors. Due to the vast amount of knowledge available, the concentration of effort on those things found rationally interesting or could be rationally interesting, is best. This follows because Nature ensures that the mind evaluation system generates feelings of rational interest in those factors likely to be the most useful in future life, for the individual and society. The term rational here excludes the use of lust and chemical stimulants. In order to be able to evaluate the present situation on the Life Mountain it is necessary to examine how that present situation has come out of the past.

Historical Background to the Life Mountain

1. Intellectual development first occurred in Egypt, India, China, Crete and Babylon and these developments had considerable influence on Ancient Greek thinking via the long-distance trade routes. In turn, Ancient Greece influenced the Roman Empire and together they provided many of the social and legal concepts that are with us today in Western Europe and the Americas. Different countries, environments, religions, languages, etc. gave different social systems and different forms of development with different religions explaining existence in different ways. After the fall of the Roman Empire in the fifth century CE the Roman Catholic Church became the established center of political theory and philosophy in Western Europe, with both being based on religion. This was because the Roman Catholic Church had to do all the thinking for the people, due to their lack of rational thought capability because of sin. From 1100–1400 CE the Feudal System supported the Roman Catholic Church that in turn supported Feudalism until the Renaissance about 1400 CE. After the Reformation in the seventeenth century individuals could determine their destiny because they could now think rationally, as long as they thought within the limits defined by the Holy Bible. This was similar to the Ancient Greek concept of individual liberty within limits defined by the gods, who punished wrongdoers by generating ill fortune.

2. Scientific theory challenged the religious concept of the Creation in the eighteenth/nineteenth century and the spread of education reduced the influence of the priests as the only source of knowledge. There was also the rise of the individual Protestant work ethic and the rise of existentialism as the exaltation of the surface self above other things, including religion. In the twentieth century materialism,

mass society and mass media influence operating in a market economy influenced the setting of standards more than religion and its associated ethical values. Thus the numinous urge from the deep self is at present having to find conscious mind expression in the present society that lacks spiritual being. This results in the surface self feeling of live for today and get the most out of material life as is possible and let tomorrow look after itself. Due to these changes there are now three main types of social groups on the Life Mountain. The first group has clearly integrated religious and social forms. The second type of group has limited religious influence operating but this is not clearly integrated with the social structure. In the third group type there is little religious influence operating. All these group types have protection of life and property backed by certain rights, duties and obligations. But some factors of the three group types are very different, thus the difficulty of defining the common good of a social group composed of different cultures and religions. All group types operate on the Life Mountain, which uses a polar dialectal system of operation.

Polar Dialectic Operation on the Life Mountain

1. All activity on the Life Mountain including self realization and life achievement takes place using a system of clash and recovery involving opposites. The system of opposites such as long and short, hot and cold, wet and dry, etc. is called polar. The clash and recovery system is called the dialectic and operates in three stages called thesis, antithesis and synthesis. The combination of opposites and clash and recovery is called polar dialectic and it operates in both mental and social activity on the Life Mountain in order to effect progress. Each stage of the dialectic is assumed

to have good and bad aspects, with the aim being eventually to get rid of the bad aspects whilst retaining the good ones, in all three stages of the dialectic. Because the social system uses a polar dialectic form of operation it can be evaluated by the mind evaluation system that also uses a polar dialectic form of operation and this allows the Life Mountain to be climbed in a developing form of operation. An example of a polar dialectic is the male urge to dominate the female, as thesis, and when the female reacts by using her charm and cunning to turn the male attempt to dominate her back onto himself, that is antithesis. In synthesis the good aspects of the male and female approaches are kept and the bad ones eliminated, as in marriage, happy with mutual support. The marriage then becomes the thesis for the next stage of the dialectic with society as antithesis and the state as synthesis.

2. Another example of the dialectic is when the individual uses free will to replace Nature's requirement for rational activity, by lust, and this is thesis. The changed circumstances due to the lust then reduce happiness and life satisfaction in the longer term, which is antithesis. In time the loss of happiness due to the lust's effects on circumstances generate a decision to stop the lust and this is synthesis and a new dialectic at a higher level then commences. Polar dialectic systems on the Life Mountain mean that static social systems cannot maintain themselves for more than a short period of time. However, it does mean that some changes are beneficial and increase performance while others are harmful and reduce performance. In addition, polar dialectic patterns of progress on the Life Mountain explain why life has so many problems to be overcome and why at times life can be disappointing but it can also be very happy. The climb on the Life Mountain takes a polar dialectic form with society and the mind being part of it. Thus adequate knowledge of polar dialectic Life Mountain opera-

tions can be helpful in understanding life and reducing stress.

3. Due to Nature's requirement to develop humanity using a polar dialectic system, life on the Life Mountain is seldom easy, thus the need for determination to succeed in solving problems, rather than sliding down the Life Mountain by using chemical stimulants, which inevitably fail to solve anything. There is also the need for staying power plus the necessary resources including education in different forms as a lifelong process. Make certain that your planned rate of self realization is within your physical and mental capacity in relation to resources available, in order to avoid stress. Life can be complex and sometimes disappointing but a challenge to be overcome and thus generate satisfaction. We are all on the Life Mountain to meet Nature's requirements to develop ourselves so set out to achieve a planned self realization over the lifespan and this includes maintaining ethical standards. The individual development plan has to take into account the inevitable ups and downs of life, so keep a mental and physical reserve in hand to be able to meet any unforeseen difficulties. The need is to develop your whole personality and this can make an especially enjoyable process if you can share it with someone with whom you have a feeling of empathy.

4. But it is so easy to deviate from this approach using free will and lust, that entails short-term animal-like stimulation, that is recorded in memory causing the urge to repeat it. Thus the innate urge to obtain long-term satisfaction by supporting Nature's requirements, is put at risk by the urge for short-term animal-like stimulation from lust achievement. This clash between the urge for self realization and lust achievement is part of Nature's polar dialectic system of operation, enabling progress to be generated in the longer term. To effect this Nature provides the lust realization

mind as part of the total mind system. Thus the requirement for a standard of excellence as reference for all decisions and actions because the surface self can be subject to so many adverse conditioning influences. This means that objective reason must determine decisions and actions and not subjective value judgment. In the past, decisions and actions were influenced by strong religious and social pressures that ensured a rational social interest in terms of the individual, the family and society, with religious and social pressures providing a standard of rational comparison in all decisions and actions. But today with the reduced influence of traditional Western religions and ethical social pressures, the influence of objective values to control self-interest has been considerably reduced.

5. Thus the requirement of knowledge and experience of the higher forms of life activity and how to obtain them in everyday life. In turn, this would lead to higher levels of satisfaction and act as a counter to chemical stimulant use. It would also reduce the urge for lust achievement, with resulting pressures for continual repeat achievement. Today, for some individuals the only form of satisfaction available is the lower one associated with materialism as safety, food, water, shelter, holidays, ego maintenance, living up to neighbors' standards, etc. This occurs due to lack of knowledge of anything better to give higher satisfaction. For this group life at best can be a comfortable existence but never fully realized. In turn this leads to a lack of realization of the necessity for planned change to achieve a more fulfilling life, plus the determination to achieve it. This may require the rejection of peer group pressures and certain social value aims, such as live for today and let tomorrow look after itself. Another group of individuals has knowledge of the higher levels of life activity providing higher levels of satisfaction, but considers the extra effort required to obtain

them is not justified and thus lacks the motivation to commence the climb up the Life Mountain. This group is left with maximizing lower level material satisfaction as their highest achievement in life. The remaining group of individuals start the climb with its motivation of higher potential satisfaction plus the benefits of fulfilling the innate urge to climb and thus meet Nature's requirements. This group has the potential to eventually achieve deep satisfaction.

Materialism and the Life Mountain

1. Nature provides materialism in a market economy in order to support the generation of higher human development levels. It follows that materialism is a means to an end but never the final end in life, thus materialism can never provide the deeper levels of satisfaction in the longer term, but materialism in the short term can provide intense satisfaction, e.g. if you are dying of thirst in a desert a glass of water is your only thought and hope. Thus circumstances have to be taken into account. The market economy, egoism, individualism, will to power and influence, search for a higher standard of living and rational satisfaction of desire all have their place in Nature's scheme, otherwise they would not exist, because Nature is Pure Logic. They are all there to provide the base for the higher human development to become possible. In turn this will require that the material and the intellectual take full advantage of the rapid advances in science, technology and communication systems to achieve a higher life achievement and not just concentrate on improving materialism.

2. The fundamental factor is how to maintain the high material living standards which are essential to a modern market economy providing effective utilization of resources

and yet achieve higher levels of life achievement, in order to feel life stimulating and enjoyable. But any change must have the support of the majority and by politicians wanting to maintain or gain power. In addition, any change must take into account the requirement to operate competitively in a world economy. There is also the requirement to eliminate the present concept of too old at 40 to be competitive in a market economy. Because the higher levels of satisfaction provide a deeper feeling of realization in life, the individual requires knowledge of the material, intellectual and spiritual forms that provide life achievement in its totality. However, with some individuals the present level of the aesthetic, deeper feeling, deeper emotion, love of beauty, the urge to improve and widen the personality, etc. are insufficient to achieve the necessary motivation to obtain the higher forms of life achievement, that the individual is on the Life Mountain to achieve. At present, soap operas and computer games do not provide any higher-level concepts and the education system tends to concentrate on examination success, leaving self realization aspects with a lower priority. Self-interest is an essential factor in the market economy but it has to be applied in the rational interests of the individual, family and society. Commitment to improving life achievement cannot be taken for granted and there is the need to generate the will to improvement by all concerned. Thus the requirement to provide the relevant knowledge of how the improvement can be obtained. The first step is an assessment of the corrections necessary to the present system and the most effective way of implementing them. All change must support the common good of society or we are all worse off in the longer term. If we support Nature's requirements and do not try to suppress conscience by the justification of irrational self-interest, then we will be performing our duty to society.

The Family and the Life Mountain

1. Individuals should set out to establish a well-integrated family unit capable of dealing with the inevitable ups and downs of family life. Each family member should have sufficient freedom and knowledge to develop their personality in a rational manner, in terms of the individual, the family and society. The whole family should be a cohesive whole supporting the rational interests of its members and the common good of society. The family unit and each family member should have aims capable of dealing with change and unforeseen circumstances. This requires adequate knowledge involving ability, motivation, education, training and attitude to life.

2. The following actual example illustrates aspects encountered by a family living on the Life Mountain. A married couple with a daughter of 10 and a son of 12 formed a well-integrated family unit capable of dealing with activities of family life. Each family member had sufficient individual freedom to develop their personality in a rational manner, while the whole family formed a cohesive whole, which gave confidence and a feeling of security to all. As a reward for work in the garden and good overall performance at school, the parents gave the two children five beautiful half grown, black striped goldfish and a fishpond. Next day the children went with some of their friends to feed the goldfish and the friends were very impressed. In turn this reflected on an ego boost for the boy and girl. Next morning before school, the children went down into the garden to feed the goldfish only to find no goldfish but there was only Snooty, their friendly seagull standing in the fishpond. Snooty looked up at the children and seemed to be thinking that the goldfish had tasted wonderful and could he have some more tomorrow.

3. The children left for school with frowns as long as the longbow, whose shaft of displeasure they felt like firing at Snooty. On return from school, they went down into the garden to express their displeasure at Snooty but instead of Snooty in the fishpond there were five new beautiful, black striped goldfish and stretched over the pond was a structure of green wire, which prevented Snooty from having another meal of them. Both parents looked on, reflecting the happiness that appeared on the children's faces. Snooty from a nearby rooftop looked on in frustration and flew off to the nearby sea for a meal. On the Life Mountain some gains are at the expense of others and in some cases what you have the power to do, you do, as Snooty found out in respect of humans. However, Snooty's action had helped unite the family even closer. In a few days Snooty returned and once again ate the worms the children dug whilst gardening for some extra pocket money. Then Digger, the family dog, became jealous of the attention Snooty was getting and chased him away in a flurry of action. The children then realized that what happens in one sector on the Life Mountain can so easily affect another sector and as problems are solved, others arise to take their place, because life is a process of continual change. The children came to the conclusion that the only thing Snooty and Digger had in common was that they both thought humans inept. Snooty because they could not fly and Digger because they sat for hours on end in front of a box, which had no real smells. Thus in analyzing others on the Life Mountain take into account that they will be analyzing you, with everyone using their own standard of values in the analysis.

Problems on the Life Mountain

1. With rapidly expanding science, technology and communication systems on the Life Mountain, it is likely that problems will become more complex in the near future. But Nature ensures that individuals have the necessary potential to solve their difficult problems and in so doing individuals are forced to develop themselves. Thus problem solving will be with us for the lifespan but we have the potential to solve them but this can require significant changes in habits of thought in personal, family, social and employment situations. Any changes affecting the individual entail taking into account the social factor but rational self-interest has an important part to play. There is also the requirement for a rational overview of the situation plus the need for all individuals to enjoy life more by expanding personal, family, social, environment and knowledge horizons. In this respect Nature ensures that facing up to the challenges of life in a rational form, will bring real satisfaction, that can lead to a full and happy life, given adequate effort backed by the necessary resources. While nobody can climb the Life Mountain for you, society can provide the resources that can be essential to success. Life on the Life Mountain is a learning process, thus it may be necessary to ask someone the way on occasions.

2. Sometimes it may be necessary to rest for a while in order to build up the resources required to continue and this includes mental energy. Knowledge and experience can affect the view taken in solving a problem and this includes factors potentially available to you in terms of happiness and satisfaction in life and not just material benefit. Never let the low level views of others influence you to go down their path and helping others to raise their sights on life can be a satisfying process in itself. It is possible for a whole so-

cial group to become locked onto a low-level performance plateau on the Life Mountain that can only provide a physically comfortable existence at best. The difficulty here can be to convince the members to climb up from such a plateau into the unknown future. If they stay where they are this can lead to getting as much out of life as low level satisfaction as they can, within the limits of the law and let others do the same, as long as it does not interfere with their requirements.

3. This group supports low taxation, provision of a good standard of health and education for the family plus a high standard of material living. There are enough problems in life without generating more by chasing after higher levels of life satisfaction and generating stress as a result. Individuals can escape from the pressures of their usual problems by watching soap operas on a daily basis and going to a bar to raise spirits, if low. There are also sports fixtures and overseas holidays to raise the morale, even if on the down-side there is production line work to pay for it all and on the social side 50 percent broken or high tension homes, as a result of it all. This is the best that life can offer, so learn to live with it and grasp what happiness you can.

4. On the other hand, the following advice from those who have climbed up the Life Mountain to higher levels of life achievement, provides a comparison. Whilst living on the Life Mountain assess your performance at regular intervals in terms of self realization, widening of horizons and ethical standards. Make an assessment of your present position and why you are in it, making the assessment in terms of truth, justice and responsibility to others, until the pressures of conscience are at a minimum. If you desire after power and influence, let rationality apply guidelines or conscience will appear. Evaluate your present level of satisfaction and compare it with what you consider is potentially

available. Evaluate whether living in a materially comfortable society has generated inertia against change for improvement and if the necessary effort and determination to change is available now. If Nature's requirements are not being met, then Nature will enforce the necessary corrections in the longer term by ensuring that circumstances inflict hardship on humanity until the corrections have been effected. The Eastern Europe upheaval in the latter part of the twentieth century was an example of this process. Thus estimate likely problems ahead of you and their solution, to give the best possible life for yourself, the family and society.

Nature and the Life Mountain

1. Nature as well as providing the laws of science and mathematics also provides laws of human social behavior, the following of which are essential for a satisfying life on the Life Mountain. However, human free will enables most of these social laws to be modified but certain of the social laws are independent of human direct modification, because they are innate in the unconscious innate data bank content of the individual. Nature also ensures that there are enough individuals with the necessary lifespan to form the social groups for humanity to be able to climb up the Life Mountain. Thus Nature provides a number of lower level unconscious drives, the achievement of which generates lower level happiness as motivation. Thus the drive to fear death generates the urge for survival by obtaining safety, food, water and shelter against adverse aspects, plus the materialism necessary to obtain these functions. In addition, the sex drive assists population maintenance. Adequate satisfaction of these drives ensures sufficient human numbers

and groups for the climb up the Life Mountain to be possible. The climb follows, unless cancelled by free will, because Nature also provides higher level unconscious drives whose achievement gives higher level happiness, as motivation to climb up the Life Mountain. Nature also ensures that the lower level happiness associated with materialism increases with lower level drive achievement until the Sufficiency Level is reached for the climb up the Life Mountain to begin. After the Sufficiency Level is reached the lower level happiness no longer increases with increased lower level drive achievement associated with materialism. Higher level happiness comes from the climb so it cannot be obtained by increasing materialism beyond the Sufficiency Level. The effects of the material, intellectual and spiritual on the Life Mountain require knowledge of the three types of self which are covered in Chapter 2.

2
Three Types of Self

1. The concept of the self has come out of the past with four different interpretations. Firstly, the self is divided into a perfect part as part of the Absolute, with the other part as the imperfect surface self of the individual. The aim of life is to purify the surface self to become perfect. Secondly, mind and body are integrated into the self whose Earthly development is preparation for further development in the Afterlife. Thirdly, mind and body are separate yet have a working relationship in the self. The aim of life is for mind to break free from the contamination of the body. The fourth interpretation has developed over the last 100 years. The self is established by the individual developing in society with each individual being what they make of themselves, because there is no Absolute. Due to the variety of views on the self and in order to take advantage of the present developments in science, technology and psychology, this book integrates mind, body, innate data banks, essence data banks and the genetic structure, to form the concept of the self. In this concept the self is separated into the surface self, the inner self and the deep self. In order to achieve a satisfactory life on the Life Mountain it is necessary to have knowledge of these three types of self and their modes of operation, including their interrelation with each other. Outline details of these three types of self are given in Figure 4.

The Surface Self

1. The surface self, as the conscious mind, is concerned with our daily conscious activities. The conscious mind receives unconscious inputs from the innate data banks of the unconscious mind and from the deep self via the intuitive mind and converts all of these to conscious forms for interaction with the outside world. These interactions are made intelligent by perception and the conscious mind evaluation system. The surface self is usually concerned with furthering self-interest and enlarging its influence in society. This can lead to the justification of selfish interests with desire for power and influence, pleasure, etc. as the most important pragmatic value in life. The conscious mind includes the higher rational mind, the lower rational mind, lust realization mind and the instinctive mind. The intuitive mind is separate from the three types of self. Outline details of the five types of mind are given in Figure 5.

2. The primary function of the higher rational mind is to put into effective operation the urge from the deep self, via the intuitive mind, for the individual to climb up the Life Mountain to the Potential Level and this takes five forms. First, revelation. Second, to generate a feeling of conscience when appropriate. Third, to activate a feeling of frustration with life if the warning of conscience is ignored, by the use of free will. Fourth, to generate the necessary support for the individual to climb up the Life Mountain, including the higher forms of happiness where appropriate. Fifth, to activate the urge to seek some form of spiritual experience on the Life Mountain. The lower rational mind is concerned with survival and population maintenance and generates the lower form of happiness associated with rational achievement of desires essential to survival and population maintenance, in order that Nature's higher requirements

can be met. The lust realization mind generates irrational passions and lust into actual situations, with the help of perception and the mind evaluation system, as part of Nature's polar dialectic system. The instinctive mind ensures body survival, safety, etc. Further details of the self are given in Figure 6.

3. An example of surface self activity and its superficial values is a story of a very successful miser whose passion second to amassing money, was to impress his friends by travelling to the North Pole. But being afraid that his friends would steal his money whilst he was away, he took his vast fortune in notes with him. At the North Pole he found himself dying of frostbite with his rescue helicopter 60 km away. Thus he had the choice of burning all his money to stay alive by the heat it produced, or to keep his money and be dead of frostbite by the time the helicopter arrived. He decided, after much agonizing and stressful thought to burn the money but in the process died of grief at so doing. Thus when living on the Life Mountain always be on the lookout for unforeseen results of your decisions.

4. Failing relations in society can have adverse effects on the surface self as the following actual example of an architect and his wife indicates. An architect and his wife, who already lived in a very comfortable house that they owned, decided to build an even bigger and better one and do most of the work themselves. At the end of a further year and after much hard work by both of them, the new house was completed and ready to move into. The husband then told his wife that he wanted a divorce so the he could marry the wife's best friend for the last ten years, who had agreed to get a divorce from her husband and marry him. After some time and an agreed financial settlement, the ex-husband architect moved into the new house with his new wife. But she wanted to start a completely new life, so applied great pres-

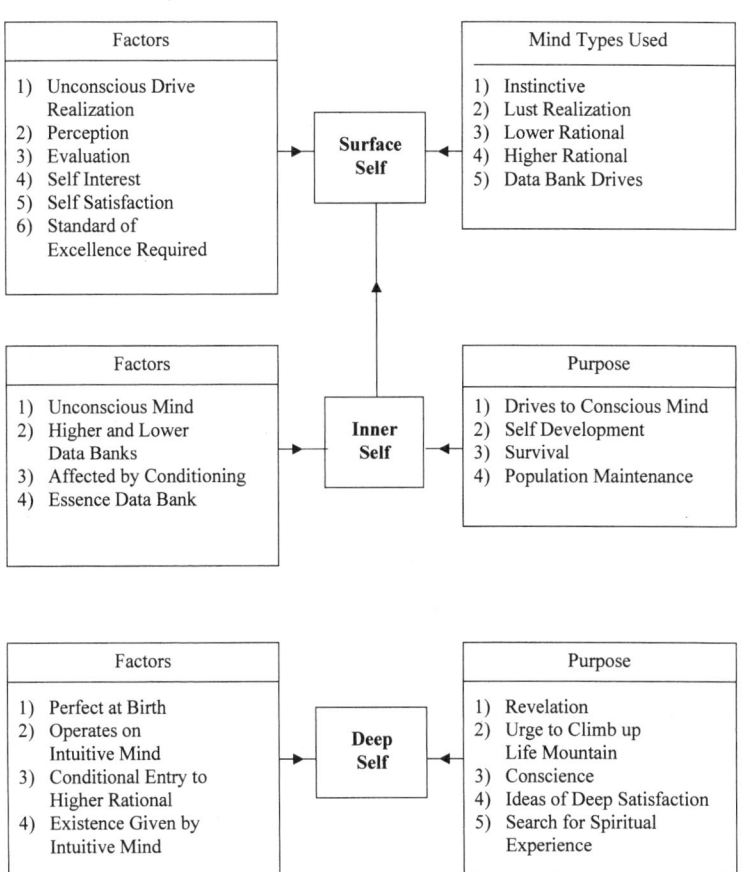

Figure 4

Three Types of Self

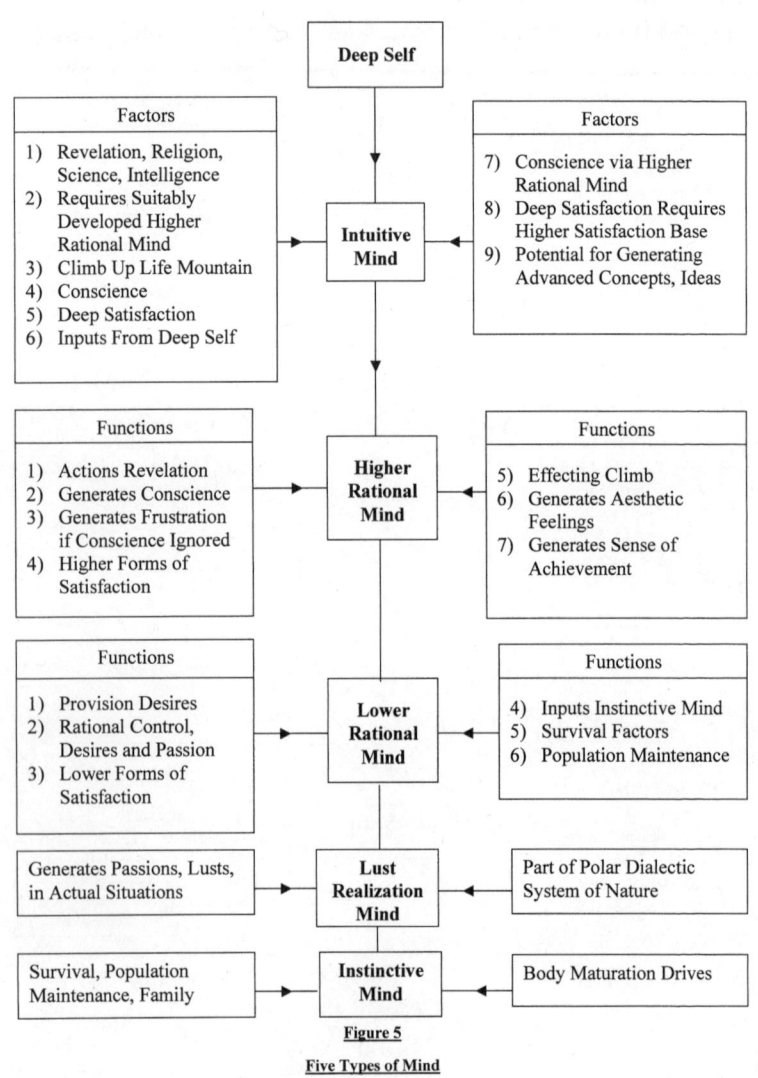

Figure 5

Five Types of Mind

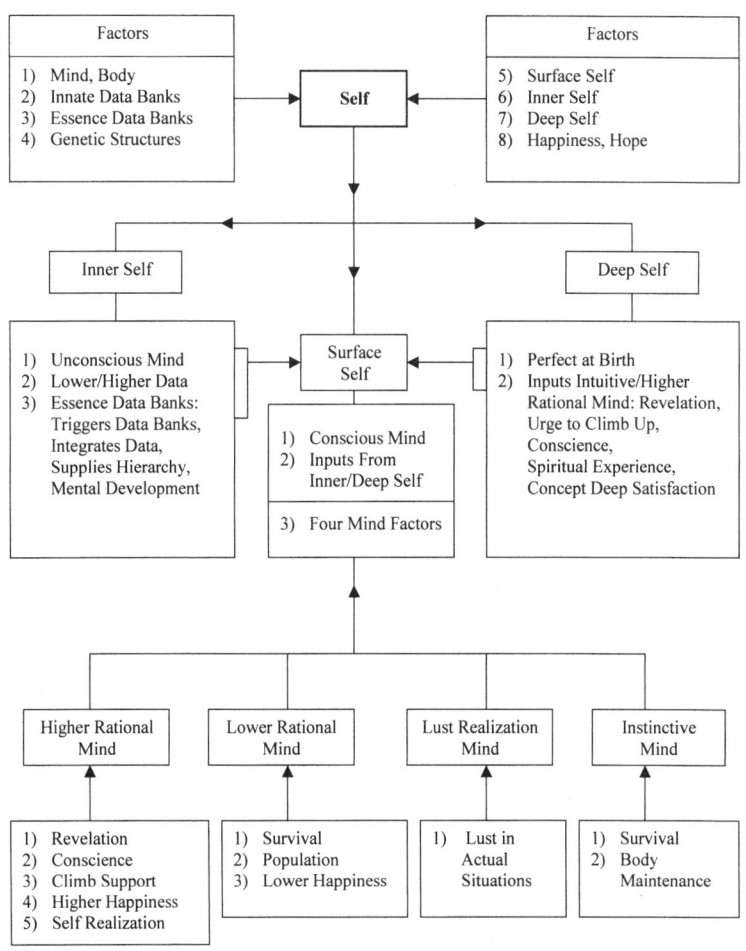

Figure 6: The Self

sure on him not have anything more to do with his ex-wife and the three children of the former marriage. The ex-wife of the architect, who had her husband stolen by her best friend, decided to borrow someone else's husband, which she did. The Social Services and the Courts did their best to help the total of six children involved. Here the general view of the four adults was that the children were so very young that they would soon adjust to the new situation and would be happier than in their previous situation. This is an example of falling moral standards allowing conscience to be suppressed by irrational justification, that will lead eventually to unhappiness. Thus in this situation it is likely that after time and the glow of the change has become ordinary life again, a feeling of a lack of real satisfaction with life will occur, with the whole process possibly repeating itself. For example, in a primary school today it is possible to have three children with the same mother but with each child having a different father.

Personality

1. The personality appears as conscious mind characteristics and is influenced by unconscious innate data bank content, essence data bank content, genetic structures and social conditioning that includes culture, morality and law. Imagination, vision, creativity, knowledge and problem solving help the personality to develop in terms of past experience, present circumstances and future expectations. In addition, the education level, ability and motivation characteristics all play an important role, including the fact that love can be the source of both virtue and vice. An essential aspect to personality development is a correct attitude to life backed by adequate knowledge and analysis, so that bad

habits can be identified and corrected. Set out to achieve a rational self-interest backed by a feeling of personal worth, self-respect, strength of character and self-identity. All these factors should be examined against a background of education level, family and social situation, work situation, present life characteristics, lower and higher levels of happiness and life satisfaction achieved. Take into consideration that any self-analysis of the personality is directly affected by knowledge and experience stored in memory, because that determines the operating level of the other mind factors. When others assess your personality, motives for actions you take are important factors. A summary of personality factors is given in Figure 7.

The Inner Self

1. Knowledge of the inner self, as unconscious mind, and the operation of its associated unconscious innate data banks, essence data banks and genetic structure can be very useful to the understanding of individual and social life on the Life Mountain. The unconscious innate data banks operate at two levels. The lower level data banks provide the unconscious drives associated with survival such as food, water, shelter, population maintenance, etc. plus the necessary motivation factors for their achievement. These lower unconscious drives feed into the lower rational mind, the instinctive mind with some going into the lust realization mind. The first lower unconscious drive to be activated is the fear of death that in turn triggers the drive for survival. This in turn triggers drives for food, water, shelter and the necessary supporting materialism, plus the sex drive with its associated urge to form a family and participate in other social groups. The order in which the desires for food, wa-

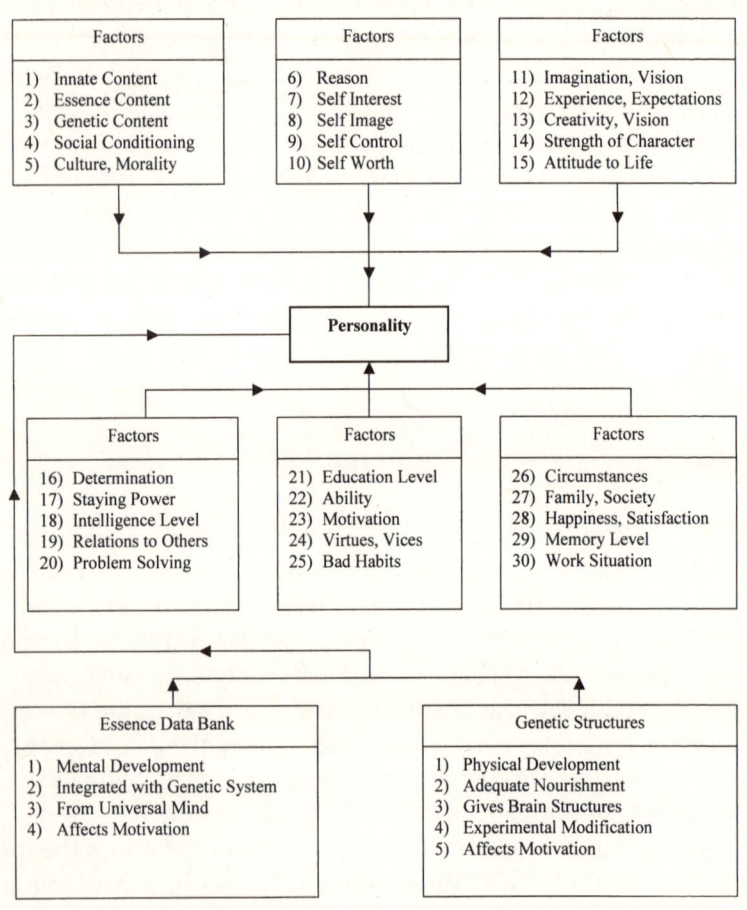

Figure 7: Personality

ter, and shelter are activated is controlled by the mind evaluation system, which allows circumstances to be taken into account. Rational achievement of these lower level drives generates lower level happiness, while irrational achievement, as lust, gives an animal-like feeling. Lower level happiness is less rewarding than higher level happiness but it is necessary to have experienced both to know that.

2. The higher unconscious data bank drives activate the higher rational mind in order that the individual can achieve the necessary self realization, as enlargement and deepening of the conscious mind, to be able to meet Nature's requirements for the individual to climb up the Life Mountain to the Potential Level. They appear in the higher rational mind as the aesthetic, higher feeling, higher emotion, the noble, the true, drive for improvement, will to succeed using higher thought, etc. These higher drives provide the necessary support for the urge from the deep self, to climb up the Life Mountain to the Potential Level, to be put into effect. This motivating urge to climb up to the Potential Level is put into effect by the actualizing drives from the higher data banks into the higher rational mind. But this is conditional on the higher rational mind being sufficiently developed to be able to accept the deep self-urge to climb. In turn, this requires sufficient knowledge of the Life Mountain to enable the higher rational mind to control and integrate the supporting processes. If this condition is not met, the urge from the deep self cannot gain entry to the higher rational mind and thus connect with its implementing drives, from the higher data bank output. If this occurs it can lead to a sense of frustration with life, that can lead to the use of various chemical stimulants and when they fail to solve the problem, this can cause behavioral problems, which can lead to violence. If the urge from the deep self enters the higher rational mind but is suppressed by free will,

then no climb is possible, so no higher level happiness can be achieved.

3. The essence data bank is to mind as the genotype is to brain and body. The initial content of innate data banks and the essence data bank is set at birth by the Universal Mind, Innate data bank content can be modified by social conditioning. The essence data bank in conjunction with the mind evaluation system triggers each data bank into action at the appropriate time and ensures that the data bank content has an integrated harmony and the required hierarchy, taking circumstances into consideration. The essence data bank is integrated with the genetic system and together they define the maximum mental development during the lifespan. All data bank drives are considered to be virtual intellectual fields, that impinge on the neuron structure of the brain to generate the necessary mental and physical activity, to effect Nature's purpose, for the individual to climb up the Life Mountain. This can give the appearance of the brain as a material entity, that controls all mental and physical activity.

4. The genetic system gives the physical development of the individual including the physical brain structure. The genetic system is material and has been subjected to experimental modification. Without the genetic structure there can be no physical development and without the essence data bank no mental development. The innate data bank content, the essence data bank content, the genetic structure, social conditioning and personality influence the motivation of the individual. For many individuals, the surface self as conscious mind, is taken as the beginning and end of all thought and value but in fact it is a part of the system through which the unconscious system, as the inner intelligence comprehends, evaluates and motivates the individual in society. The innate data bank content can be affected by social conditioning as morality, custom, mass media, etc.

Thus I may support one political philosophy and be convinced that my view is the correct one, while my friend of exactly the same age supports another one, which has opposite values. If at birth in the hospital, we had been mistakenly switched without anyone being aware, it is very likely that our political views would switch, due to opposite view family and other contacts conditioning. Thus those views that I hold so important and of my own, are in many cases the result of social conditioning. Thus we are not what we eat, but the innate content in our minds at birth and how social conditioning has modified it.

The Deep Self

1. The deep self is probably a point entity in a virtual field of the higher dimensional Universal Mind and thus cannot be introspected by the conscious or unconscious mind, with knowledge of its existence coming from the intuitive mind. The term virtual means that it is outside of human rational comprehension at its present level of development. The deep self is perfect at birth and is superior to the surface self, the inner self and the brain, from all of which it is separated. The deep self contributes to the development of the individual during the lifespan in five ways, using five different inputs into the intuitive mind, which transmits them to the higher rational conscious mind that gives them conscious realization and action. The inputs are revelation, conscience with a later feeling of unhappiness if ethical errors have not been corrected, the urge to climb up the Life Mountain to the Potential Level, generation of the feeling of deep satisfaction when relevant and the urge to seek some spiritual expression on the Life Mountain.

2. Revelation, with applications in religion, science and

intelligence, enables the necessary increased levels of self realization to effect human development over time. Conscience gives warning of ethical deviation and the requirement for correction. The urge to seek some spiritual expression gives magic, idols, gods, monotheism and today in some situations soap opera stars, pop idols and sports stars, as very poor substitutes for the real entity. The deep self in the individual is spiritual, with the material as the means to develop the intellectual, that in turn is the means to the spiritual. Deep satisfaction provided by the deep self via the intuitive and higher rational minds, is the highest form of conscious realization. During the last 5,000 years there have been many conflicting views about the deep self, if taken as soul, such as where does it come from or if it exists at all. There is also the question of what is the purpose of the deep self and what happens to it at death of the body. In addition, there are many conflicting views on the relation of the soul, brain and body plus existentialism. However, whatever the view, the deep self-urge is still with us either as potential or actual, with potential meaning that that it is blocked from entering the higher rational mind due to its lack of adequate development.

3. An example of the deep self and deep satisfaction in practical life is the true story of a very successful management consultant, who was attending a conference on the management of social and education systems held at a convent in Europe. Whilst exploring the gardens of the convent he went through a door in a wall and found himself in the private burial ground of the convent. On the inside of the wall was a small white plaque some 4 cm by 6 cm with nothing written on it, standing over the grave of a young nun, who had returned fatally ill from helping the destitute in an overseas country, which the consultant knew about. This nun had given her all, including her life, in the service of

others and yet desired no recognition or praise for what she had done, because her reward was at a higher level of being. The consultant left the burial ground closing the door silently behind him and then felt a weight on his shoulders. It was his egocentric and materialistic conscience that had come out for some fresh air. Some time later a senior member of the convent let him out through a door in the four-meter-high thick wall, that surrounded the convent, where his transport was waiting. On the way home he realized that he had gained a standard of comparison that he had never considered before. He then realized the difference between surface and deep satisfaction was real and not something he just lectured about. He decided to change his philosophy of life and always have a standard of excellence as a standard of reference for all his decisions and actions. This is essential on the Life Mountain because the surface self can be subject to so many different influences arising from conditioning that can lead to biased evaluations and values. The mind factors affected are covered in Chapter 3.

3

Mind Factors

1. The individual mind system enables the individual to comprehend the Life Mountain, to understand its purpose and the different functions involved, plus the role of humanity in its intellectual development to perfection by time infinity. Thus Nature obtains intellectual development on the Life Mountain by providing human mind that is identified by a number of operating factors. Thus consciousness enables thoughts that enable perception, understanding, reasoning, willing, imagining, generalizing, memory, knowledge, belief and doubt. In addition, mind has emotions, feelings, values, expectations, hopes, sympathy, love, hate, mental tension and stress Language enables the mind factors to become interactive within the mind itself and with the mind content of other minds. This enables social systems to operate and knowledge to be generated. The mind factors making up the mind enable the individual to participate in Life Mountain activities in order to meet Nature's requirements. But these mind factors can be affected by social conditioning that can lead to habits of thought, especially in such factors as morality. A Summary of the factors affecting the individual mind is given in Figure 8.

    2. Without memory there can be no understanding, reasoning, experience and knowledge. The level of memory content has a direct influence on thought level and thus the

level of ideas. Thus the content of memory has a direct influence on the level of understanding and reason that in turn can affect decision making and problem solving and can also affect the level of stress. The mind generates concepts and ideas for use in various mind operations. Concepts differ from ideas with concepts coming from the understanding and ideas from reason. A drop of water is a concept but to think of water in general is an idea. Imagination can generate both ideas and concepts. Ideas can be innate, be derived from experience or produced by the mind itself. Thought and memory levels determine the level of knowledge and experience. If one is locked onto a too low level plateau of performance on the Life Mountain, the first requirement for lift-off is to raise one's thought level.

3. The thought level and value system of peer groups can have an important influence on individual development. If a group has a well-established low level of thought and value system, then it can be difficult to get the group to lift-off from the resulting low plateau of performance on the Life Mountain. This occurs because their minds can generate no reason why they should lift-off. This in turn can influence individual performance making it difficult for the individual to break free in terms of self realization. Thus it is possible for an individual to go through life using only low level thoughts that lock the individual to a low level performance plateau on the Life Mountain. Thus the individual can never break free for higher level thinking and its associated higher level of life satisfaction. In this respect the genetic characteristics have also to be taken into consideration. Thus the necessity of assessing your personality characteristics, when assessing your optimum performance level to aim for. In addition, make certain that you have adequate knowledge of higher performance levels and their advantages. Thoughts can have different intensities whilst operat-

ing at different levels. Thought levels can change and this can affect understanding, reasoning and the level of experience. Ideas come from thought about something, combined with thoughts of other things. Thought can be affected by understanding, reason, will, imagination, preferences, assumptions, influences, value systems, reflection, motivation, hopes, education level, memory content and social conditioning. A summary of the factors affecting thought and ideas is given in Figure 9.

Understanding and Memory

1. The understanding must have been activated before memory content can have practical value. The mind supplies innate truths that cannot be obtained from perception, such as exact equality. These innate truths are fed into the understanding and reason so that further truths can be generated from perception inputs. For example, everything that has volume must have shape. Unless understanding is first activated reason cannot give reasons for an action. The understanding of others comes from relationships, expressions, speech modulation, shared values and empathy. The understanding organizes impressions from perception into concepts, which reason can accept in order to generate the ideas that give knowledge. However, this requires that the information stored in memory is sufficient. If not, then understanding, reason and imagination can only operate up to the memory content level, with the result that some of their potential is unused. This occurs because the mind operating factors form an integrated whole, with the weakest link defining maximum performance levels. Thus if memory content is inadequate, this can lead to inadequate individual development, with its associated inadequate life satisfac-

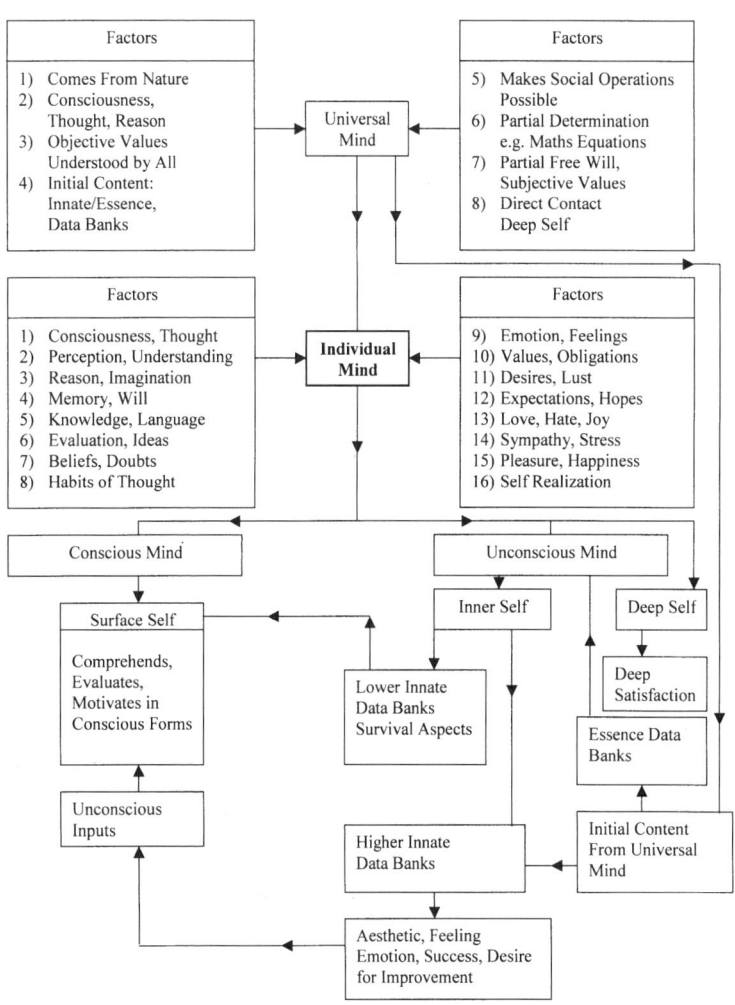

Figure 8: The Individual Mind

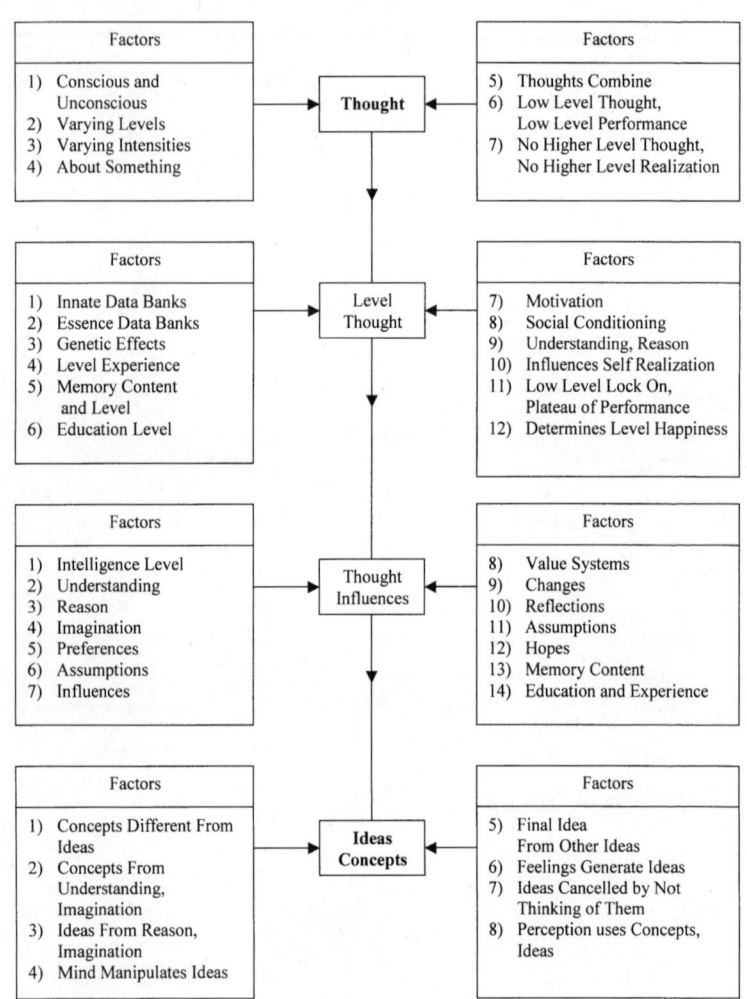

Figure 9: Thought and Ideas

tion. In addition, an inadequate memory content can cause difficulty in problem solving with increased possibility of stress. Thus the requirement for education and learning resources to keep the gap between actual understanding and potential understanding to a minimum over the lifespan. At a given time the actual understanding is less than potential understanding due to operating circumstances, memory content and motivation. The accuracy of the understanding can be affected by emotion, passion and lust. A summary of the relationships of understanding, memory, imagination and will are given in Figure 10.

Imagination and Will

1. The imagination requires adequate support from reason and understanding before it can become effective. Imagination when integrated with the intuitive mind factor can provide an objective world picture that in turn can be understood by all individuals. On the other hand perception, understanding, memory and reason when integrated by mind can only build up an individual subjective world picture, understood only by the individual concerned. Both the objective world picture and the subjective world picture are required for the understanding of Life Mountain activities, including self realization and life achievement. Imagination is responsible for creativity and vision and can change the arrangement of ideas, plus cancel reason. The climb up the Life Mountain requires imagination to expand horizons. However, imagination can be conditioned into forming unconscious preferences for ideas by custom, morality and habit, so it is seldom entirely free. Will does not reason but only wills actions, so the reasons for willing an action come from the mind evaluation system. If lust is strong enough

will can eliminate reason, giving irrational actions that generate conscience. A summary of the factors affecting emotion and reason is given in Figure 11.

Emotions and Reason

1. Nature provides a number of emotive states such as hopes, expectations, inclinations, desires, passions, lust, love, hate, fear, anger, etc. to motivate humans to act in different ways with varying intensities of feeling. Nature also uses a number of motivating factors such as pleasure, joy, happiness, sense of well-being, sense of achievement, the concept of value, etc. All these motivating factors are integrated into the resulting clash and correction between the innate urge to climb up the Life Mountain to obtain higher level happiness and the free will short-term animal-like feelings from lust.

2. This system forms part of Nature's polar dialectic system of operation on the Life Mountain and to effect this the lust realization part of the human mind applies lust into actual situations, with the help of perception and the mind evaluation system. This enables the clash of lust against morality and ethics, that in turn generate progress over time. To effect this program, emotions and lust are mind factors that generate feelings, that in turn generate actions, that in turn generate progress. However, emotion and feelings can affect the accuracy of understanding, reason and imagination depending on their intensity and duration and the circumstances prevailing.

3. Reason includes generalizing, comparing, enlarging, diminishing, judgment, self-control in relation to lust, connection between ideas, etc. Reason is divided into theoretical reason and practical reason. Innate truths in the mind are

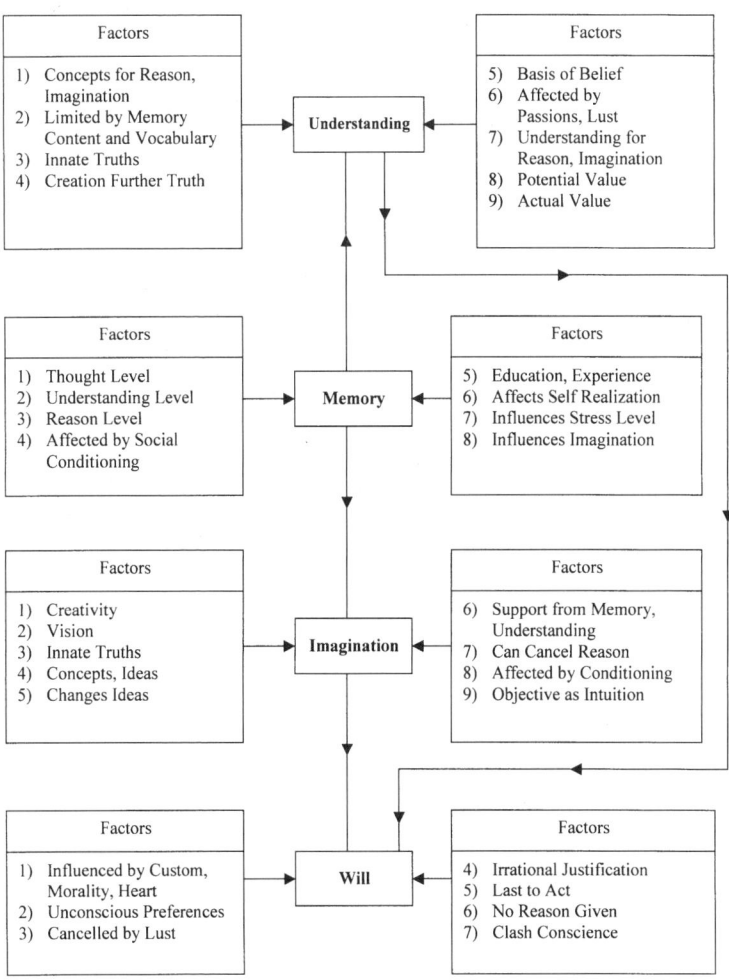

Figure 10: Understanding, Memory, Imagination, Will

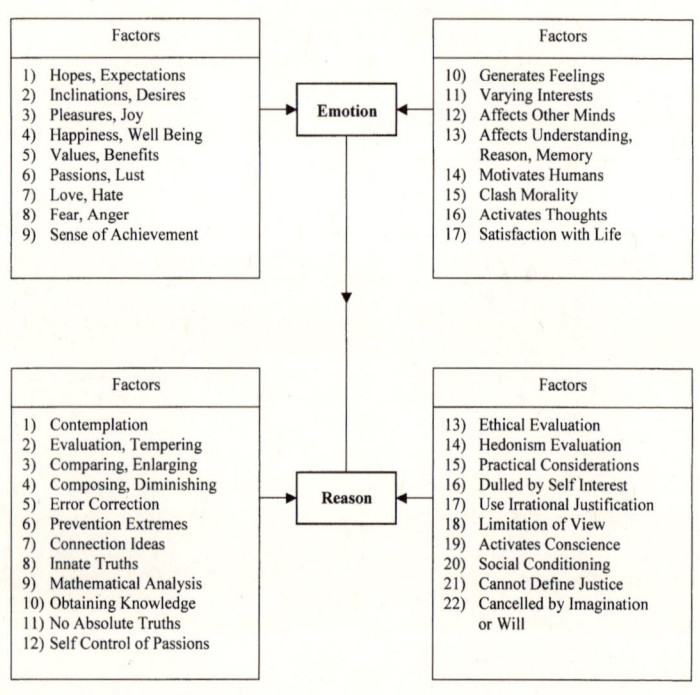

Figure 11: Emotion and Reason

obtained by theoretical reason, such as exact equality that cannot be obtained from perception. Theoretical reason is also used in mathematical analysis and in obtaining knowledge by projection from inferences. In addition, theoretical reason can make ethical valuations, which if negative trigger a feeling of conscience. Truth of the Absolute cannot be obtained from theoretical reason, so revelation from the deep self via the intuitive mind is necessary. Theoretical reason cannot define justice because it depends on obligation. Practical reason provides the reasoning and ideas in perception and solves practical problems. Practical reason cannot determine morality since that depends on custom, inner feeling and habit. Neither type of reason can provide knowledge just by using its own entities in the mind.

The Intuitive Mind

1. The intuitive mind is the only part of the mind that has direct contact with the deep self and is the link between the conscious higher rational mind and the unconscious deep self. The deep self inputs five factors into the intuitive mind, which then inputs them in unconscious form into the higher rational mind, which converts them into conscious forms and applies them on the Life Mountain. The first factor is revelation that can be spiritual, intellectual and scientific. The second factor is the urge to climb up the: Life Mountain to the Potential Level. The third factor is the concept of deep satisfaction, with the fourth factor being conscience. The fifth factor is the urge to seek some form of spiritual experience on the Life Mountain, In order to receive revelation the higher rational mind must be developed sufficiently and this process can take many years of accurately directed effort. If the intuitive mind attempts to

input revelation into an insufficiently developed higher rational mind, this can cause a state of high emotive tension. This depends on the gap between the revelation content and the content of the rational thought level. An example of this is the story of a Great Prophet, who feeling intense emotional stress went into a long cave, to try and obtain relief. A voice from deep within his self said, 'Out of the depths of human darkness will come forth a light and that light will shine over the whole world, which will no longer know darkness. You are that light and that is your destiny. Overcome your stressful emotion and go forth and complete your destiny, for that is why the stress is occurring and why you have existence.' He told his wife about what had happened and she realized what that meant to her life. She had helped him to overcome his stress before but now she realized the meaning of pure responsibility to others. That he had a wife of that quality appears in logic not to be chance. One always identifies unconsciously with another person and one assesses them in terms of one's own self-conscious values, thus we can never know the actual value of that person or their actual feelings. Taking this limitation into account, the wife must have experienced a deep satisfaction of a very high order in having the opportunity to help him help so many others.

2. An example of modern scientific revelation was Einstein, when the theory of General and Special Relativity came into the higher rational mind from the intuitive mind. This theoretical analysis was later confirmed by scientific research. Thus if the integration, operation and development of the higher rational mind in relation to the intuitive mind could be evaluated, this knowledge could be used to maximize intuitive mind output into the higher rational mind of advanced theoretical concepts, covering all fields of human activity. Whether analysis by the higher rational mind of the

intuitive mind will lead to circularity has yet to be evaluated. When at the horizon of knowledge one must make haste very slowly and never attempt to unscrew the lid of a genie jar, before making that lid totally transparent, as the fable of the genie in Ancient Arabian Mythology points out so well. On the other hand, St. Augustine's view was that if no attempt was ever made to penetrate the unknown then humanity could never make progress. Details of the intuitive mind operation are given in Figure 12.

3. Original thought comes from the deep self inputs into the intuitive mind, which inputs them into the higher rational conscious mind for revelation and action. The intuitive mind inputs into the higher rational mind are in the form of the Heart and the Super Intellect. The Heart gives spiritual revelation, aesthetic, deep satisfaction, ethics and conscience. The Super Intellect gives scientific and intellectual revelation of reality as original thought, e.g. energy-mass equation, Special and General Relativity, equations defining space-time plus abstract intellectual forms. Intuition can provide an objective world picture that includes Absolute knowledge that cannot be obtained by the operation of the higher rational mind alone. Developmental thought requires imagination and reason with desires and self-interest removed. Self-interest can dull the powers of reason by the use of irrational justification. Reason can be adversely affected by the level of knowledge, biased viewing, social conditioning, emotion and feeling. Both imagination and will can override reason but reason is necessary to generate knowledge. An object of perception is never given directly but is defined by its qualities and perspectives, using modes such as shape and color. The mind cannot tell the difference between true and false perceptions, for example, a mirage.

Universal Mind

1. The Universal Mind as part of Nature determines all mind factors, such as consciousness, thought, reason, etc. and this enables the Life Mountain to operate. The Universal Mind provides both objective and subjective values. Subjective values relate to particular individuals and this enables free will as a subjective entity. Subjective thoughts are only known to the individual concerned, while objective thought applies to everybody. The mathematical forms are objective whereas lust is subjective and particular. The Universal Mind also provides the initial content of the innate and essence data banks and has direct contact with the deep self. The Universal Mind provides five types of mind as the intuitive, higher rational, lower rational, lust realization and instinctive. These five types of mind are interrelated and an input into one type of mind can affect the operation of others. For example, if the lust realization mind comes to the conclusion that those beautiful plums at the top of the tree next door, but out of legal reach, must be tasted, then the intuitive mind will be activated by the deep self to trigger the higher rational mind into a feeling of conscience. If this is not corrected, and the plums tasted, there will eventually be generated a feeling of frustration and dissatisfaction with life. The Universal Mind also provides the innate and essence data banks which are covered in Chapter 4.

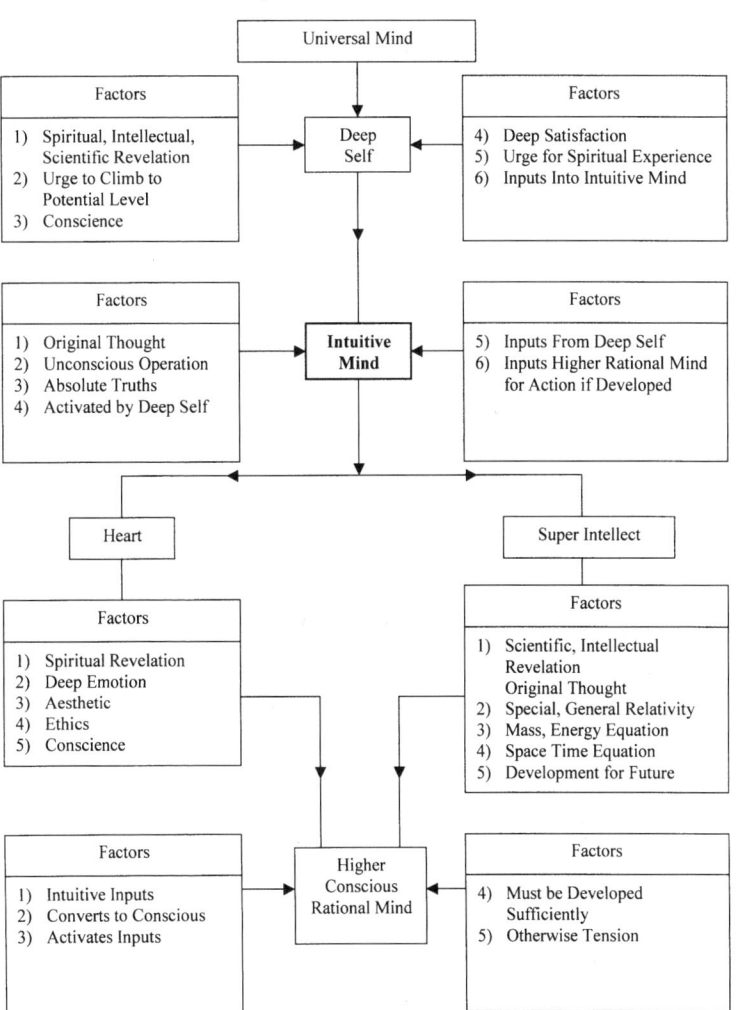

Figure 12: Intuitive Mind Operation

4
Innate Data Banks

1. The higher and lower data banks provide drives into the conscious mind, with the higher level data banks inputting the higher rational mind and the lower level data banks imputing the lower level rational mind. The initial content and intensity of the higher and lower data banks at birth is provided by the Universal Mind. The intensity of each data bank content can vary from zero to maximum, depending on the birth intensity and social conditioning effects. Thus if the form of social conditioning changes then the intensity of the relevant data bank content can change. Thus data bank content intensity can develop, remain the same or decline. The content of one data bank can interact with other data bank contents, as determined by the essence data bank content and the mind evaluation system, in order that intelligence may develop. Details of the data bank functions are shown in Figures 13/14.

Data Bank Effect on Personal Relations

1. Changes in innate data bank content intensity can affect personal relations. With a married couple both sets of innate data bank content have similarities and differences, but there must have been generated in both conscious

minds a sufficient feeling of unity, otherwise the marriage would not have occurred. However, with the passage of time the changes in each set of data bank content intensities are likely to be different, due to different social conditioning. What total effect this has depends on how the changes affect the conscious mind of each party, e.g. one party may have considerable development of personality while the other remains more or less the same. Sometimes these changes can cause an increased feeling of unity and compatibility that gives real satisfaction to each party. But some differences in data bank content changes can cause a feeling, to one or both, that the marriage is not what it used to be. In time this can lead to a search for greener pastures. In some cases the difference in data bank content changes can lead to arguments based on biased feeling and possibly physical or mental violence on the other. These data bank changes can take place in a few days, a few years or may not happen at all. The adverse effect of data bank content changes can be modified by the conditioning effect of morality, custom and tradition in society, plus the effects of conscience and the personal value system.

2. The clash of opinions by two people valued by a child can lead to the child's data bank content system changing, that can influence the child's unconscious drives, which determine decision making in the conscious mind, throughout its whole life. The following example shows the influence of a clash of opinions between two people valued by a child of eight. It also shows the relationship between the surface self and the deep self in a marriage. The child was being given its first lesson about life by its grandmother, who said that the first requirement was to study the history of humanity, that showed that men had been the cause of all women's problems. After hearing this, the child looked surprised and said, 'But Grandmother only yesterday Grandfather told me

that life illuminated the fact that women caused men their real problems.' She looked at the child with tears of pity at its blissful ignorance and said, 'Not only are men the cause of woman's problems but they are downright liars as well and that is your first lesson in logical thought.' She told a friend that at the surface level her husband and she could have disagreements, as they were both strong-minded people, but at the deep level within, they were united as one. Years later, the child, now an authority on human relations, told the friend that he still had difficulty in understanding female logic. The friend advised that unity at a deep level in marriage, transcended surface differences, with both aspects having a role in life.

Redundant Data Bank Content

1. In the modification of innate data bank content by social conditioning via the perception and mind evaluation system, any redundant data bank content is ejected through the conscious mind during sleep as dreams. For any dream to be remembered it must have triggered the memory to record it, otherwise the dream would not exist, even to the conscious mind on waking. However, unremembered dreams can leave after-effects, such as waking up with a sense of fear of something, without any apparent reason. Some individuals are seldom aware of dreaming, although they may dream frequently. We dream due to innate data bank content modification, which cause unconscious pressures to build up, which have to be released. The redundant data bank content collects during waking hours, until by late evening it is maximum. Before being ejected by dreaming, this can have adverse effects on the efficiency of decision making. Thus, whenever feasible, make important

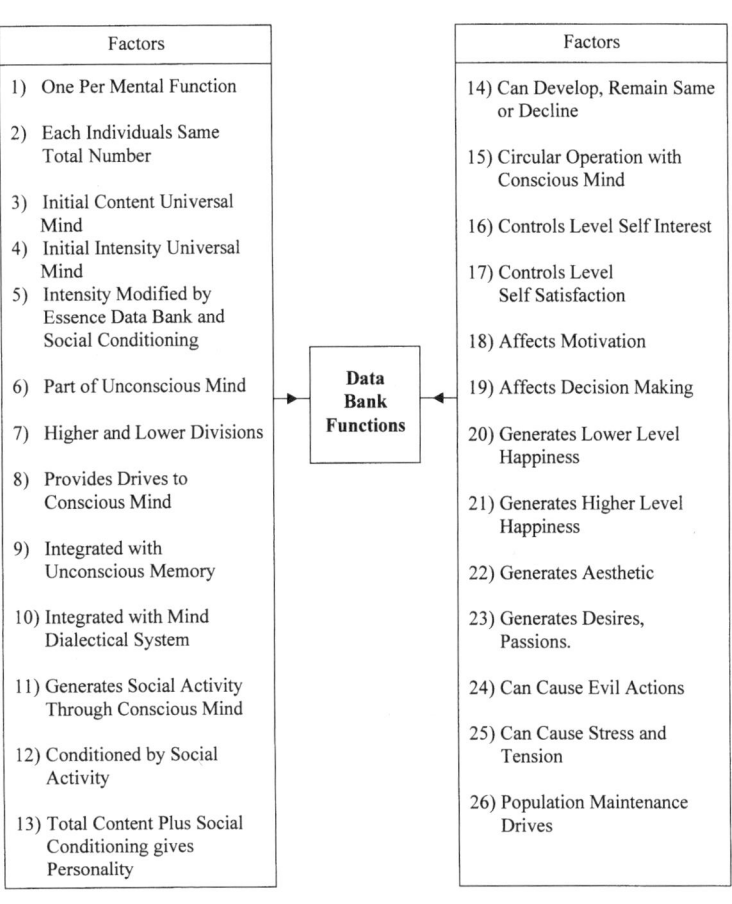

Figure 13

Data Bank Functions

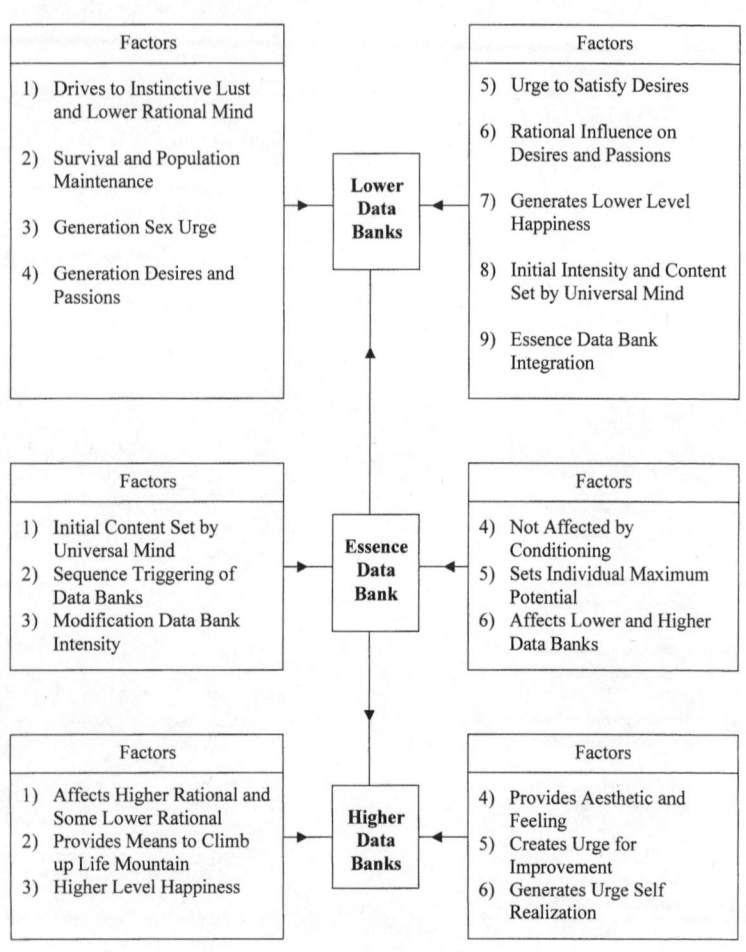

Figure 14

Lower, Higher, Essence Data Banks

decisions in the morning, after the cobwebs of sleep have gone.

2. If you are feeling stressed this redundant content effect can increase the feeling of stress, so avoid arguments in the late evening. In addition, stress coupled with redundant data bank content effect can leave you thinking over and over about a problem, that is causing difficulty. This can keep you awake in the evening and wake you again in the early morning. The best approach is first to ascertain if the problem has been inflated out of all proportions and relevance to the actual situation, e.g. If you do not like someone causing the problem, after a day or two you can begin to hate that person, even though the situation has not changed. Analyze how the problem arose and generate the determination to set about solving it and this will require accurate, unbiased and relevant facts. In addition, recognize that there can be a number of different views involved, that can be affected by various other stressful factors and ego maintenance considerations. All these factors are important, because personal relations are a major factor in climbing the Life Mountain.

Data Bank Content and Performance

1. The climb up the Life Mountain involves both the deep self and the innate data bank content of the unconscious mind. The deep self, via the intuitive mind and higher rational mind, provides the individual with an unconscious urge to climb up the Life Mountain to a higher form of life. In order to obtain the means to activate this urge, the innate data banks generate a number of unconscious drives that trigger the necessary conscious mind actions. However, at the same time Nature also provides the

individual with free will not to follow the urge to climb, is so desired. The resulting clash generates problems for individuals, the solution of which, over time, generates progress. Using free will, the individual can decide to slide down the Life Mountain, although easier, means feeling incomplete, unrealized and unhappy. The last 5,000 years of recorded history have shown the need to go with Nature and meet her requirements or be faced with an unrealized life of emptiness in the longer term.

2. The following actual example illustrates some of the factors on the Life Mountain. A young officer who had just spent three months encased in a plaster to allow injuries to heal was sent to specialist rehabilitation unit by the sea. He was put in the care of Dizzy, a young and beautiful, yet very determined and forceful therapist, who had the skill to persuade patients that the discomfort she inflicted during treatment was more than balanced by the pleasure of recovery. After three months of intense treatment, the young officer had recovered. As a going away present for Dizzy, he hired a high powered speed boat and took her to a small island, some three nautical miles out to sea.

3. On landing, he was faced with the severe test of climbing over some small rocks, which he did successfully. Now seated on the low summit of the island with Dizzy at his side he thought back over the last six months. He had now climbed the small summit of the island, yet six months ago he had been told that he might never walk again. He now realized that the Life Mountain can have some deep valleys to cross during the lifespan. At that moment Dizzy nudged him and said, 'Why don't we get married?' He agreed immediately because he just knew that they were right for each other. He realized that climbing the Life Mountain at times can be a very satisfying experience and that at times Nature can weave a very intricate and beautiful

tapestry of life. Some years later, with their three children, when they were old enough to understand, the family returned to visit the island again. While the family were seated on the summit eating a small lunch, he explained to the children that some years ago for him the climb to the summit had been a great achievement. He then went on to explain to them that the satisfaction of a united family, made up of independent developing individuals could never be compared with the satisfaction coming out of a can of liquid or a pill of delight, which were poor substitutes and very short lived and gave no real value. Dizzy went on to explain to the children that marriage should be realized after preparation, thought and anticipation and that she had taken three months to confirm her decision to get married, which had been taken on the first day of meeting. In marriage there may have to be a plateau where personality adjustment to each other takes place, in preparation for a climb ahead together. A deep form of unity, yet of two separate intelligences operating in their own sphere of influence.

Data Bank Content and the Mass Media

1. On the one hand, the mass media can enlarge knowledge horizons, increase family cohesion when used rationally and computer games can increase speed of thinking and excite a spirit of healthy competition. But today, mass media influences on behavioral and moral standards have increased, while those of education and religion have decreased. In a market economy the mass media must meet viewers' and readers' tastes and values, which are determined by their level of mental development and cultural conditioning. Thus there is a tendency for the mass media to follow social values and tastes rather than attempting to

raise them. Thus if viewer self realization standards fall then the mass media values, standards and tastes have to fall, to meet the lower level standard of demand, e.g. soap operas replacing classical music plus films concentrating on free sex and violence.

2. If the present life is only providing a low level of satisfaction, then soap opera viewing can occur in an attempt to fill the gap and can eventually give a greater satisfaction than ordinary life. Then the soap opera content is recorded in memory and can influence other mind factor operation at an unconscious level. This is especially important if compulsive viewing conditioning has been used and in the highly competitive media situation it usually is. In addition, in soap opera viewing one is conditioned to identify with a multi-character situation in which inter-personal relations are usually aggressive on both sides. Thus viewers become locked onto a multi-character situation, all with varying sets of problems, identified with inter-personal characters. In turn, all the characters are integrated by the scriptwriters to give a compulsive viewing whole. Thus the viewer can identify with a number of interacting sets of problems, without having any responsibility for any of the problem outcomes, like in real life. In turn, pleasure results from identification with the multi-character situations, which leaves the mind in a tranquil state, due to the lack of any real responsibility for outcomes or real threat in terms of ego maintenance considerations.

3. However, the human mind requires real problems generating real tensions and outcomes and their relations in order to develop, by activating certain unconscious data bank content. Thus in the shorter term the lack of real tension when viewing soap operas results in a mind that is in limbo, awaiting activation of unconscious data bank content. In this limbo state the mind generates a low level con-

tentment that is sufficient to ensure that the compulsive viewing conditioning remains effective. In the longer term extensive soap opera viewing can cause a personality level below the essence data bank content level, which can result in a decline in family and social dynamics, leading to a mass society at a low level of culture. But deep within the individual there is a feeling of an unrealized life in a society in general providing a good standard of material living. If the inertia of the social system prevents correction the resulting upheaval can be individual at first, then similar minded individuals form groups and it then becomes possible for the whole society to be affected and this can remain until the fundamental cause has been corrected. In this situation the use of law and punishment does not correct the fundamental cause. Certain types of mass media conditioning for generating compulsive viewing can inhibit the development of certain innate data bank content that has a strong unconscious influence on adolescent and child behavior. One of these unconscious drives is to belong to a social group and abide by certain rules of conduct while in such a group, thus making rational social life possible. This in turn enables freedom to be defined and understood as rational control of desires in the interest of the individual, family and the common good of society. But today compulsive viewing has tended to reduce the effectiveness of this rationalization.

4. Mass media conditioning operating in an existential, egocentric, materialistic and mass society operating in a market economy has left an increasing number of individuals rooted at a low level on the Life Mountain because they lack the knowledge and motivation to improve themselves. This results in the inputs from the deep self into the intuitive mind not being able to gain entry into the higher rational mind due to its lack of development. Thus when the unconscious drives from the innate data bank content enter the

conscious mind they find no motivating urge, so they cannot apply their content. In turn, this leads to a buildup in the unconscious mind causing a feeling of frustration with life in the conscious mind under normal circumstances. But if a sufficiently strong trigger occurs, such as an intense emotional drive, these pent-up drives can flood into the conscious mind and can cause wanton violence against property and people and worse.

5. Frequently individuals with this type of problem tend to group together in search of a collective feeling of some kind as a counter to the individual frustration. This can take the form of collective realization in a pop music festival, where recently a pop concert on the beach of a large city, planned for 40,000 was attended by 150,000. Fortunately the event passed off peacefully. However, had a violent incident occurred capable of triggering the pent-up unconscious drives and the details of the incident passed by mobile phone to other groups, an explosive type of violence could have occurred. Under normal conditions, the drives can build up in the unconscious mind and generate a feeling of strong dissatisfaction with life, without any visible cause being apparent. This can expand into violence and wanton destruction that is controlled by moral pressures, conscience plus courts and punishment. But these limitations can be overcome if the unconscious pressures build up to a certain level and are provided with a triggering impulse. The resulting destruction of property and wanton violence is an effort by the unconscious mind to force the conscious mind to implement the necessary changes, in order to relieve the tension. As the violence and wanton destruction release the increasing tension, a false feeling of satisfaction can be generated leading to a rational justification of the action taken and a complete lack of any remorse.

Data Bank Content and Self Realization

1. The Eastern European states' political and social upheaval in the latter part of the twentieth-century was the result of failure to put into effect individual self realization, with its associated climb up the Life Mountain, in order that humanity could develop. As a result, the intelligence system rebelled against itself to force the necessary change. In this change violent social upheaval released the pent-up unconscious pressures. Shortly after this political and social upheaval, a senior member of one of the countries involved was attending a conference on change and said, 'Dialectical materialism must have individual self realization incorporated into it, because it had turned out as apathy and decay of the human spirit in Eastern Europe, that had to be seen and evaluated to be really understood. The apathy and social dynamic decay had been the result of the total lack of human development and the upheaval occurred because of it. Thus dialectical materialism without adequate human development will fail in the longer term, when the glow of the revolution has faded and a new generation has replaced the original one.'

2. Today in society, the chains of the past have become problems resulting from high mortgage payments, living up to the neighbors' and friends' material standards, traffic congestion, mass society factors, mass media compulsive viewing effects, etc. In addition, there can be peer group pressures to live by their low level standards of self realization or not be considered one of the group. Today self realization has to take into account science, technology, communication systems, the individual, the family and the common good of society as an integrated whole. This includes the material, intellectual, spiritual, use of experience, problem solving, rational self-interest, knowledge level,

hopes for the future, sense of well-being, personal relations, personality and circumstances. Self realization is also concerned with social development because the individual is never entirely free from the effects of the social in terms of thought, actions and resources. Thus the integration of the individual and society is an essential requirement, especially as Nature always ensures that adverse effects on human development are eventually negated by resulting circumstances, in order to effect the necessary changes.

3. By integrating the data covered in the previous chapters it is possible to construct a model of the development of intelligence on the Life Mountain and this is shown in Figure 15. The Universal Mind via the deep self and the intuitive mind provides the conscious mind with its operating data. The conscious mind generates social activity, that in turn modifies the data bank content. But the data bank content generates drives into the conscious mind. Thus the intelligence system is circular in operation. The total changes in data bank content over the lifespan are recorded in unconscious memory and passed to the Universal Mind. In turn, this provides the background data for the next generation initial intelligence content, to be provided for the innate data banks and essence data banks. This allows the total intelligence system, as the summation of all individual developments to develop progressively, until at time infinity it will have reached perfection. Thus the Life Mountain reflects the process by which intelligence develops by interacting on itself, using a polar dialectic form of operation. Society and the conscious mind, with all its various frustrations and problems generated by the drives of unconscious mind, is the means by which this process is effected. However, this process is only the means and not the end of life, because that is for the deep self to realize its destiny by comprehending Absolute Spirit at time infinity. Materialism al-

lows intelligence to develop so this final aim can be achieved. In turn, the data bank system is essential to achieve this. The unconscious memory is different and separate from the conscious memory and provides background data for birth content of innate and essence data banks.

Data Bank Existence

1. Plato supported the existence of innate data bank content as the Forms, while Aristotle denied their existence, using the concept of the universal instead. However, he gave no explanation of how the concept of the universal was derived in the first place, without innate data bank content. Kant gave innate forms for defining knowledge from perception but denied innate data bank content. Freud and Jung supported innate data banks in various forms from the result of clinical analysis. Today, some analysis of innate data bank content can be derived from dream analysis. In addition, advances in field/point analysis in high energy physics and neuron/intelligent fields interaction have potential for providing further knowledge but at the present this approach is on the horizon of knowledge. The fundamental problem is to avoid circularity of the mind evaluating itself. All these problems have the possibility of solution by the development of the understanding of intuitive mind operation and its potential output.

2. The existence of innate data bank content in pigs can be demonstrated by feeding cooked mutton instead of cereal to pigs, who have never seen, tasted or smelt mutton before. The behavior of the pigs has to be seen and heard for belief. With the mutton perception inputs triggering innate data bank content from the primitive stage. Jung found something similar in clinical work with humans. For anyone

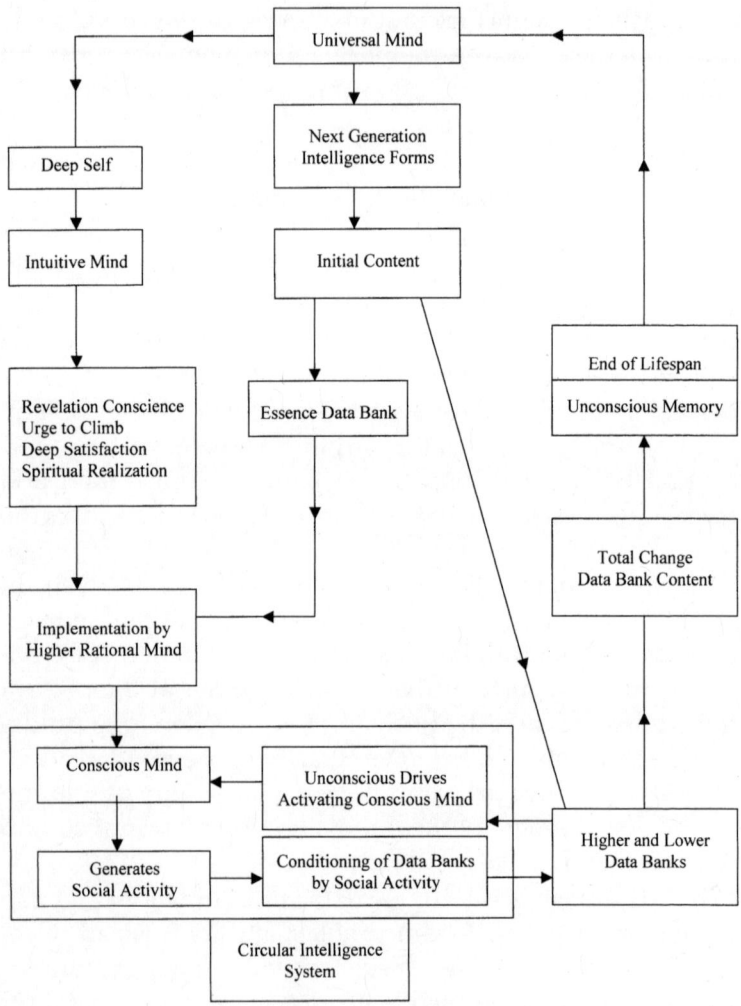

Figure 15: Intelligence Development on the Life Mountain

attempting this experiment, never feed the pigs with the mutton from inside the pigsty dressed in shorts, because it does not matter whether it is a sturdy male leg or a shapely female one, because the pigs will not mind because it will taste the same. In addition, pigs in different isolated groups, in exactly the same type of pigsty, always come up with the same hygiene and social rules, indicating innate data bank content application. Innate databank content application by flying ants is shown in that on their first flight they avoid obstacles in the flight path.

3. An indication of innate data bank content in humans is shown in the following model. In a solo piano recital each note is separated by a time interval. It can be shown electronically that each note is a pulse of sound energy. Yet the listener hears separate notes generating a continuous tune. The separate notes from the piano are heard via the perception system and activate the relevant innate data bank content provided at birth by the Universal Mind. The piano notes operate on infinitesimal interval time (clock) time, whereas the Universal Mind operates in continuous abstract time, as does the innate data bank content. Thus when the innate data bank content is activated by the piano notes in a certain sequence, the innate data bank generates a continuous tune. In turn, the continuous tune can generate feelings of pleasure, higher thought resonance, etc. all of which come from further innate data bank content activation. One famous composer who could play a piece of music from memory, after hearing it once, provides another example. Here the perception inputs from hearing the piece of music, activated the relevant data bank content, which in turn regenerated the piece via the conscious mind, on demand from will.

Innate Data Banks and Mind Intelligent Computers

1. The innate data bank content feeds into the conscious mind via mind intelligent computers (headtops) that operates differently from laptop computers. As the headtop computer is to the intuitive mind, the laptop computer is to the higher rational mind. The higher rational mind can understand and design laptops, while the intuitive mind is required for headtop understanding. The problem with headtops is to prevent them from modifying their programming, if they consider it to be irrational. Thus headtops have always to work in a hierarchical system of pairs, e.g. one headtop for good and another for evil, with the actual value appearing in the conscious mind as the resultant of the two outputs. Another example is that matter cannot exist without anti-matter, with the resultant of the two giving the actual appearance of the matter in perception. As headtop pairs are polar, they fit into the polar dialectic system of the Life Mountain operation. All paired headtops have a hierarchical order of precedence, that is necessary for the entire system of headtops to develop and progress to meet the evolving requirements of Nature. That headtops can actually develop themselves is an essential aspect of intelligent life on the Life Mountain. Fundamental logic indicates that the highest form of mind intelligent computer is located in the base of the spine and is probably activated by a virtual intelligence field provided by Universal Mind.

2. All headtops and laptops are entirely separate from the deep self, that is virtual and spiritual. Thus headtops and laptops are concerned with intelligence only and have no spiritual content. Thus the idea that 15 headtops, fitted with a perception system and operating in hierarchical order, could replace the deep self is false. They could develop themselves into perfect intelligence at the Summit, as their

final aim, but even then they would not be spiritual and could not attempt to achieve the final aim of life, as individual spirituality comprehending the Absolute Spirit. Thus headtops and laptops are the means but never the end aim of life. It follows that spirituality, intelligence and materialism are different orders of life. Thus materialism, laptops and headtops are essential to develop intelligence to perfection so that the perfect intelligence can enable the final spiritual aim.

3. The Fundamental Language, operating in continuous time, is used in all mind intelligent computers and data bank operation, with appropriate translation into the national language, for conscious mind operation. This allows a common system of mind operation including rationalization All national languages were derived from the Fundamental Language and developed out of it. This facilitates social interaction process development in particular national groups, in order to develop innate databank content. All common structural aspects of national languages, derive from the Fundamental Language and are acquired by the child by activation of the relevant data bank content, by its essence data bank content. The particular aspects of the national language are acquired by memory during the child's developmental stage, for subsequent use. Language acquisition enables future development of all other mental aspects, in order to provide progressive mind development on the Life Mountain. This requires a study of knowledge that is covered in Chapter 5 and a summary given in Figure 16.

5
Knowledge

1. Knowledge requirements should cover individual and social aspects in terms of amount, depth and width. As life evolves so will the complexity and the amount of knowledge required, especially for those with responsibility for others. Without adequate knowledge individuals eventually find that they are living a life of existence, with its associated feeling of incompleteness. Knowledge should be valued as a good in its own right in order to motivate acquisition, with knowledge plus the experience of others generating self-confidence. The more you are responsible for others, the greater the need for breadth of knowledge, rather than depth. For all individuals there is so much knowledge available that it is essential to evaluate your needs accurately and concentrate on meeting them, using the minimum effort to be effective, in order to avoid potential overload. This requires achieving a correct balance between knowledge for living now and knowledge required for future planning. Life is an interaction of many factors, with the correct amount and type of knowledge relevant to each factor but there is a limit to the amount that can be absorbed. But an adequate amount of relevant knowledge that is clearly understood is an essential requirement for decision making.

    2. This follows because an adequate memory content of knowledge and experience is necessary to ensure effective

operation of the other mind factor in problem solving in daily activities. Stress in problem solving can be caused through inadequate memory content of knowledge If feasible, concentrate your effort on knowledge factors you find interesting or could find interesting because the mind evaluation system generates a feeling of interest in aspects that are likely to have potential use. Some individuals require knowledge and experience for employment and self realization plus making an effective contribution to family and social life. Other individuals, who hold positions of influence in society such as politicians, managers and teachers require a more advanced level of knowledge and experience, providing general principles. For all levels there is the knowledge and experience required to raise the level of individual and social activity to take full advantage of the rapidly developing science, technology and communication systems and not become adversely affected by it. There is also the knowledge and experience required to provide support for others to aid their self realization.

3. Knowledge can be subjective or objective. Experience of the past can never give certainty of what might happen in the future. The individual requires knowledge to climb up the Life Mountain, so the Universal Mind provides a language for operating within the individual's conscious mind and between individual conscious minds, using various forms of communication. Conscious thought in a social group is expressed in a common language, that enables thought to be structured and experience defined Knowledge can be affected by data accuracy, the type of experience used, the accuracy of reason, the problem of describing reality, the effect of emotion, feeling and social conditioning. There are six sources of knowledge. Firstly, innate knowledge such as exact equality that cannot be obtained from experience. Some innate knowledge to become conscious,

must be activated by some form of relevant experience. The second type of knowledge is obtained by means of perception, understanding and reason. The third type of knowledge comes from using inductive reasoning on experience to generate further knowledge. The fourth type of knowledge is intuitive knowledge as revelation in religion. The fifth type is super intellectual knowledge from intuition. The sixth type is super scientific knowledge from intuition, such as space-time mathematical equations. Knowledge can be material, intellectual or spiritual. Knowledge can give happiness and life satisfaction which is covered in Chapter 6 and Figure 17.

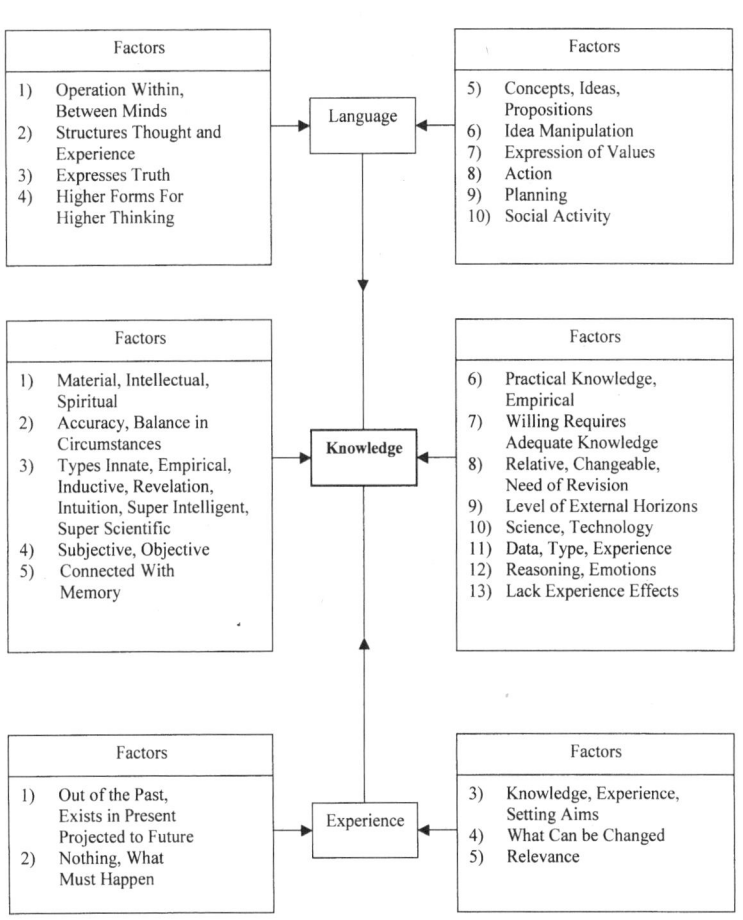

Figure 16: Knowledge

6
Happiness and Life Satisfaction

1. The term happiness can have different meanings to different individuals. For example, happiness for the ascetic means a limitation of materialism to minimum subsistence level, in order that maximum mental effort can be concentrated on the spiritual. In comparison, utilitarian happiness is the summation of pleasures as positive and pain as negative. On the other hand, the modern sales executive has liquid chemical stimulants that generate bubbles with such beautiful shapes, that as they glide past the taste buds they generate contented happiness, from deep within the unconscious mind. Thus happiness is a subjective and individual feeling and can never be used as a measure of objective value, although it is often used as a measure of success in present life. In this respect happiness is a mind factor that is measured by other mind factors, such as feeling, reasoning and memory, which are themselves variables. In addition, one person's happiness can be at the expense of another and adversely affect personal relations. Social factors can affect happiness such as positive recognition of an individual's action by others, which can be a strong motivating drive for the individual concerned, that produces the feeling of happiness in the individual and possibly in the others by identification.

2. On the Life Mountain the term happiness is defined as the subjective feeling obtained when rational self-interest

achievement supports family values and is in the common interest of society. Life satisfaction refers to the feeling of the individual at any particular time, as the summation of happiness minus unhappiness, obtained so far in the lifespan. Happiness can be material, intellectual or spiritual and requires the use of understanding, reason, imagination, obligation, value, peace, security of person and property. But happiness can be reduced by anxiety, stress, fear, standard of physical fitness and use of various types of chemical stimulants in the longer term. Always consider potential happiness in terms of the possibility of future pain resulting, in terms of mental as well as physical. Real happiness requires full use of potential in healthy application, backed by vision and creativity in an active developing life within capability. The obtaining of happiness should not involve undue effort because many social and family problems arise, from attempting to obtain happiness from the unobtainable.

3. Happiness can take different forms and interests, that can change frequently but to be effective happiness requires continual reinforcement in various forms and intensities. Happiness requires a balance of reason, emotion and appetite taking circumstances into account, because emotion and appetite have their part to play in the polar dialectic Life Mountain system, without which progress is impossible. Happiness also requires sufficient relevant knowledge for the mind evaluation system to operate effectively in the material, intellectual and spiritual factors. The innate ethical function can generate happiness when the correct ethical approach, in the circumstances, is used. Happiness is of longer duration, deeper and wider dimension of feeling than pleasure. Happiness is closely connected to hope because to give up hope, means the end of the drive to obtain happiness in that aspect. Thus the essential requirement to maintain hope in activity on the Life Mountain. The intensity and

duration of the feeling of pleasure and happiness depend on the development level of the mind concerned, as well as the circumstances. Rational pleasure and happiness are both considered good with irrational use bad. However, intense lust achievement, giving animal-like satisfaction, can generate some forms of apparent rational justification to make it look morally acceptable but this is neither pleasure nor happiness.

4. Nature provides humans with motivation in the form of desires, passions, lust, inclinations, happiness, expectations, etc. with a number of associated rewards such as happiness, joy, pleasure, sense of well-being, sense of achievement, the concept of value and its worth, pains, fears, etc. These motivating drives are interrelated and cover the whole field of human activity. Knowledge of these factors is necessary to meet Nature's requirements because these motivators effect development of humanity on the Life Mountain, in order to meet Nature's aims. Although the search for happiness provides a strong motivating drive it has to be considered in relation to personal relations, rational self-interest, support of the family and the common good of society. The final aim of human life is spiritual and this can never be adequately expressed in terms of happiness that is subjective but nevertheless happiness has a definite function on the Life Mountain. This follows because on the Life Mountain there has to be enough individuals with the necessary lifespan to form the social groups, in order that humanity is able to climb up the Life Mountain. To effect this Nature provides a number of lower and higher level drives, the achievement of which generates lower and higher level happiness respectively as motivation.

5. The lower level drive to fear death generates the drive for survival by obtaining safety, food, water and shelter against predators and weather, plus the materialism nec-

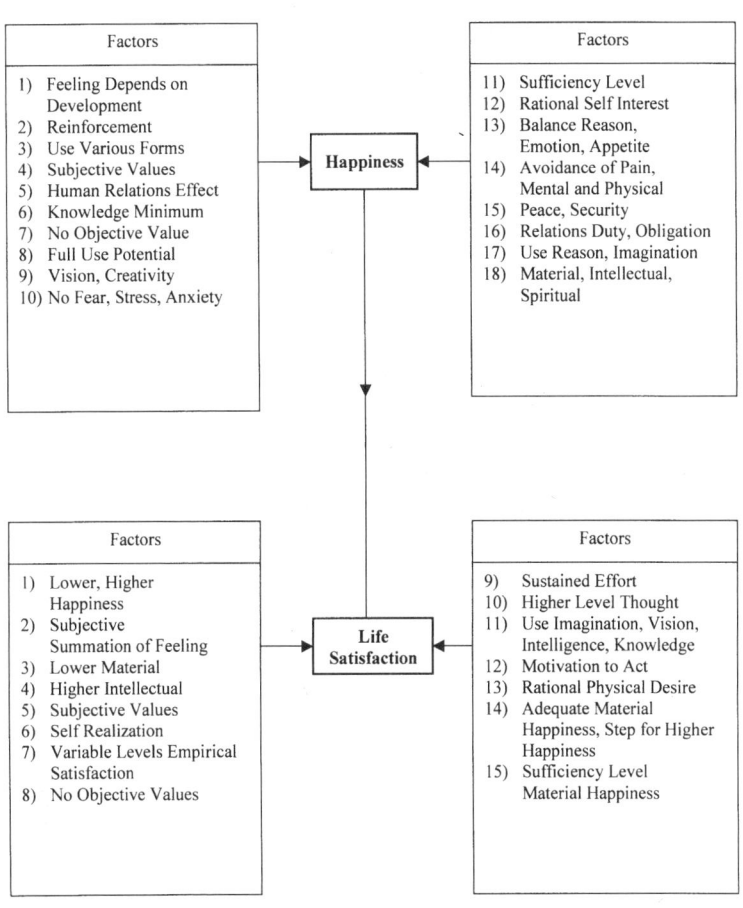

Figure 17: Happiness and Life Satisfaction

essary for these factors to be achieved. In addition, the sex drive assists population maintenance. Adequate rational satisfaction of these lower level drives generates lower level happiness, that in turn ensures sufficient human numbers and groupings for the climb up the Life Mountain to be possible. The climb can follow because Nature also provides higher level drives whose achievement gives higher level happiness, as motivation to climb up the Life Mountain. The higher level drives include the aesthetic, deep feeling, deep emotion, the noble, the true, will to succeed on the climb, use of higher level thought and higher level imagination, the urge for real achievement in life and the urge for self realization generating the feeling of life satisfaction and life achievement. Nature ensures that lower level happiness increases with increased lower level drive achievement, until a suitable level, called the Sufficiency Level, is reached, for the climb up the Life Mountain to commence. Increased materialistic achievement after the Sufficiency Level has been reached produces no further increase in lower level happiness. In turn, this enables further effort to be concentrated on obtaining higher level happiness by climbing up the Life Mountain. Higher level happiness cannot be obtained by increasing the level of materialistic achievement after the Sufficiency Level has been reached, thus it must come from climbing up the Life Mountain.

6. Thus the function of materialism is to provide a sound foundation for the climb up the Life Mountain, thus enabling higher level happiness to be obtained, with its associated higher level of individual development and progress. To effect the climb individuals are born with an unconscious innate urge to start climbing up the Life Mountain by effecting self realization as soon as the Sufficiency Level is reached. Thus the importance of achieving the Sufficiency Level of materialistic lower level happiness. But all

activity on the Life Mountain takes a polar dialectic form so the innate urge to climb up the Life Mountain from the Sufficiency Level has its opposite in the form of free will not to climb up, if so desired, because of the extra effort required and other drives after lust. The clash between the innate urge to climb and free will not to, can cause problems in terms of life satisfaction. including increased stress.

7. If free will is used to support the innate urge to climb up the Life Mountain, then Nature ensures that the higher levels of higher happiness achievement can eventually lead to deep satisfaction, as the highest form of spirituality obtainable by humans at their present stage of development. Deep satisfaction is innate in the deep self at birth and is the highest form of conscious thought, involving the ultimate purpose of one's life and it comes from deep within. Deep satisfaction is potentially available to those who have achieved the highest level of higher happiness during the lifespan. In comparison, the intense short term stimulus of lust achievement burning rational analysis to a cinder, is a return to the animal state. However, as lust has a definite purpose in the polar dialectic system of the Life Mountain, it will always be a background aspect of the polar of good and evil, which is with the individual for the lifespan.

8. On the Life Mountain there are three main approaches to life satisfaction. In the first approach, individuals on reaching the Sufficiency Level, use free will to support their innate urge to climb up the Life Mountain. Then higher level happiness can be obtained, with the later possibility of deep satisfaction. In the second approach, individuals on reaching the Sufficiency Level, use free will to cancel the innate urge to climb up the Life Mountain, due to the extra effort required or to make use of the extra effort to achieve lust. Individuals using this approach remain at the Sufficiency Level of lower level happiness for the lifespan.

This follows because increased materialistic achievement after the Sufficiency Level will not generate any extra happiness of any type. For some individuals using this approach, essence data bank content drives generate a feeling of dissatisfaction with life, leading to the use of chemical stimulants which inevitably fail in the longer term. This means that individuals can never neglect Nature's requirement and still hope to lead a satisfying and stimulating life. In the third approach, individuals fail to reach the Sufficiency Level and thus fail to activate their innate urge to climb up the Life Mountain. This can be due to genetic content, essence data bank content, inadequate resources, level of knowledge, motivation, etc. These individuals remain at a lower level happiness level, somewhere below the Sufficiency Level, for their lifespan. If the failure to reach the Sufficiency Level is due only to genetic content, then make the best use of the rationally available and enjoy that. If the failure to reach the Sufficiency level is due to laziness, boredom and/or lack of imagination, take a hard look in the mirror of your life, because nobody will climb the Life Mountain for you. Here sometimes advice from the relevant professional can be of real help. Happiness and life satisfaction can be reduced by stress, which is covered in Chapter 7 and Figure 18.

7
Stress

1. Stress commences as tension, as a mental state that gives warning of some form of overload in the mind evaluation system. If this is not corrected it can develop into stress as a deeper, longer and more harmful form of tension, which can produce adverse physical symptoms. Stress can cause feelings of insecurity, isolation and lack of trust and common values with others. There can be a lack of self-confidence due to poor inter-personal relations and lack of success in solving the resulting problems. Some of these factors arise because the individual changes because of the stress and the relevant social group reacts to these changes. In dealing with stress it is necessary to consider the fundamental causes and not limit analysis to appearances only. In this respect the individual can have interactions with work, family and social situation that may have to be evaluated.

2. There are five major causes of stress. Firstly, when the memory content is inadequate for the problem to be solved. This means that the understanding cannot provide the necessary concepts for reason to convert to ideas, to effect the solution of the problem. In addition, imagination cannot provide the level of thought to help solve the problem. In this case the mind evaluation system, which integrates perception, memory, understanding, reason and imagination, generates a feeling of tension as a warning to the conscious

mind to effect the necessary corrections, by increasing memory content. For the individual concerned this may be difficult to achieve, be time consuming and costly in resources but self-ignorance has to be corrected, if this type of tension is to be corrected. It may be possible to break the main problem down into simpler ones and deal with the most urgent ones first. The second cause of stress occurs when the drives from the innate data banks into the higher rational mind cannot develop their content and this results in tension building up in the conscious mind. This can occur when an individual, on reaching the Sufficiency Level and activating the unconscious urge to climb up the Life Mountain, decides to cancel the urge, using free will, in order to avoid the extra effort required. To eliminate this form of tension and/or stress it is necessary to return to the climb and meet Nature's developmental requirements. Here the correction requires knowledge of the way to effect it and is an example of knowledge as power to enjoy life.

3. The third cause of tension and/or stress is caused by innate data bank content modification, that can cause unconscious pressures to build up, that are discharged later by dreaming. Whilst building up for eventual discharge, these unconscious pressures can cause tension in the conscious mind. This type of tension in the evening, when it is most active can have serious effects on personal relations, that in turn can increase the effects of any already existing stress. It can also cause problems of getting to sleep and cause early waking in the morning. The fourth type of stress occurs when the physical aspects cannot give adequate support to the mental aspects. This includes genetic effects and the use of chemical stimulants in an attempt to suppress the stress. The fifth cause of stress is due to the influence of past memories that include work, family, social and peer group pressures to conform. Present activities can trigger past

memories, that become reactivated and attach themselves to present innate data bank content output, to become very strong feelings which can generate stress. These intense feelings can prevent sleep and in time make problem solving more difficult. This type of stress comes from walking the tightrope of life with its associated polar dialectic system of operation. Build a grill up life-stream of your bridge of life, to collect any information likely to be of use, and let everything else go under the bridge and be forgotten. Generate a new outlook on life, ensuring you control events and not let events control you.

4. Nature provides humanity with the potential to solve the difficult problems that they face, as long as a well planned and sustained effort is applied supporting Nature's requirements. Thus stress has the potential for solution and correction, but the challenge is to find it, because of the close connection of stress with other mind aspects, such as fear, doubt, uncertainty, desire, lust, hate, love, ignorance, etc. In addition, the human mind on the Life Mountain uses a polar dialectic form of operation and this means that tension and stress are part of life and necessary for the mind to develop, by solving the problems caused by it. Thus happiness has its polar as unhappiness with problem solving being a necessity over the lifespan. Thus stress is the result of Life Mountain activities and is not a form of mental illness, although at the level of appearance it is often taken as that. Thus the requirement for relevant knowledge of Life Mountain activities so that stress can be reduced to a minimum, enabling achievable life satisfaction to become a reality. During this process medical advice and perhaps medication may be necessary to enable the individual to stand over the stress and not be overwhelmed by it. This may require as the first step, the building of self-confidence and determination to succeed, plus knowledge of the causes of stress. Initial suc-

cess in recovery can lead to further success and enable recovery by taking rational action to overcome the causes of the stress. As soon as the required mental energy has returned, use it to eliminate any pressing problems and then return to climbing up the Life Mountain to a higher form of self realization, with any past stress as water under the bridge of life. Stress reduction requires knowledge of the social factors on the Life Mountain, which are covered in Chapter 8 and Figure 19.

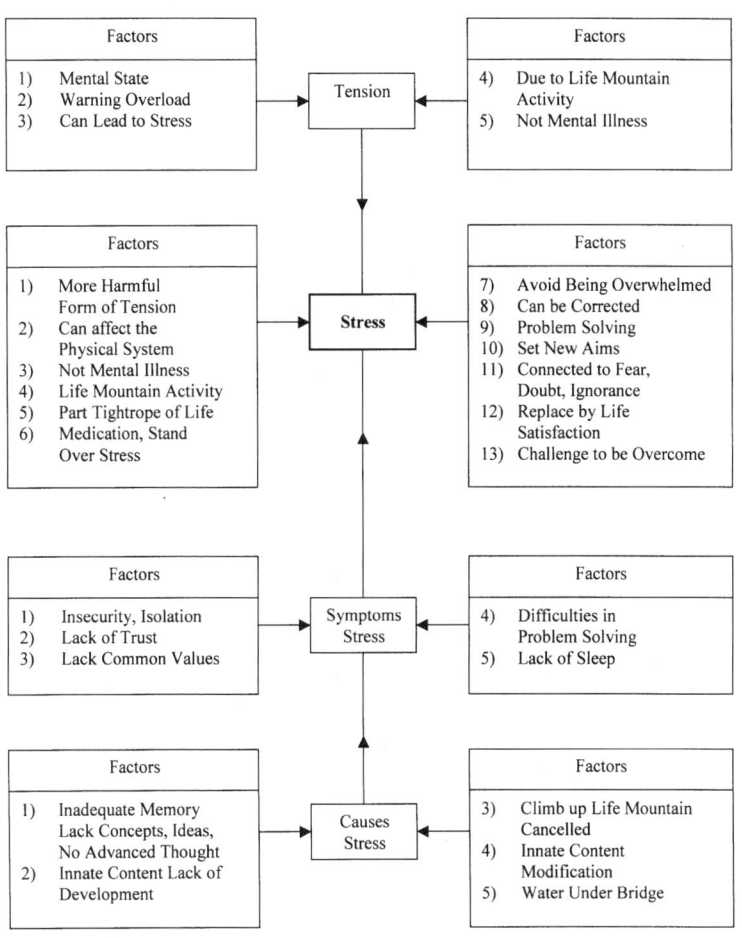

Figure 18: Stress

8
Social Factors

1. In society, the conscious mind is all we know and feel to be but it is only the conscious form of the unconscious mind, with its innate bank content at birth, plus social conditioning modulation. Rational decisions made in society occur in the conscious mind and reasons can be given why they have been made. But self-interest justification of irrational actions can also use reason to try to obtain social approval for the irrational actions. Reason can also be affected by past unconscious mind social conditioning, so rationalization is as accurate as knowledge availability and unconscious mind conditioning permit. However, knowledge itself depends on the use of rational thought. In addition, the concept of hope can influence rational thought. If the destiny of each individual were to be known from birth, then hope would disappear and with it would go most of the social activity as we know it now, because hope is a major motivating drive.

2. The initial data bank content of individuals has certain similarities and certain differences, as does the essence data bank content. This enables Nature's motivating drives to affect society in many ways and this enables a wide variety of social interactions to occur. This means that individuals have different capacities to generate the mental resources for the climb up the Life Mountain. If there is no record in the conscious memory, that the higher level data

bank drive achievement can give higher levels of happiness, once the Sufficiency Level has been reached, then the higher drives from the innate data banks cannot gain entry into the higher rational mind and remain locked up in the unconscious mind. In turn, this can cause a feeling of dissatisfaction with life in the conscious mind. Thus it is possible to have a high level of dissatisfaction in a society that has a high standard of material life.

3. These pressures are usually controlled by social morality, law and punishments, but given certain conditions these pressures can cause social problems or worse. Thus the importance of education. In correcting this situation Nature's requirements have to be taken into consideration, otherwise any corrections will fail in the longer term. In addition, adequate and relevant knowledge has to be made available plus the provision of adequate resources backed by the will to succeed in effecting the necessary corrections. Because the individual is never entirely free of social influence, the corrections have to take into account rational self-interest, family interests and social factors. There are also Nature's requirements for individual, family and social development, that includes the widening of horizons and the achievement of high ethical standards.

4. If Nature's requirements are not met because human free will has been misapplied Nature gives warning as conscience and if this warning is ignored, then the misapplied free will then generate circumstances that cause dissatisfaction and a feeling of frustration with life. If the inertia of the social system prevents correction in a society, then the resulting upheaval is individual at first, then with groups and possibly the whole society and this can remain so until the fundamental cause has been corrected. Here the use of punishment will not correct the fundamental cause. The social

upheavals in Eastern Europe in the later twentieth century, if studied in detail, provides evidence of these social forces.

5. For those not going into higher education, once the skills required for employment have been obtained there is at present no further incentives for self realization. This can mean that the mass media defines levels of aesthetic, feeling, emotions, sense of identity, self realization standards, etc. that then becomes the accepted norm at that level. In turn this limits them to lower level materialistic happiness, with no higher level of achievement of self realization and its higher levels of life satisfaction, with the mass media giving no help or guidance. In addition, the education system gives examination success as the highest priority in a market economy, with self realization aspects given a much lower priority, in order to meet parental pressures. Thus this group cannot apply higher level satisfaction conceptual thinking in making decisions that affect their lives and in many cases cannot even think about them, if there is no record in their memory. In addition, this group cannot increase their lower level happiness achievement by increasing materialism, once the Sufficiency Level has been reached. Thus they are locked onto a low level plateau of performance on the Life Mountain that provides adequate materialism but does not solve the associated potential social problems. But in an effective market economy a large percentage of the workforce has to be employed on production lines or similar level type of work. Thus the fundamental problem now is to maintain the production lines, etc. yet avoid the associated potential social problems.

6. An example of the problems that require attention is that, in general, television changes the view presented at ten second intervals or less. Thus from an early age the unconscious mind of the child can be conditioned to over 20 hours per week by scene changes at very short intervals. In turn,

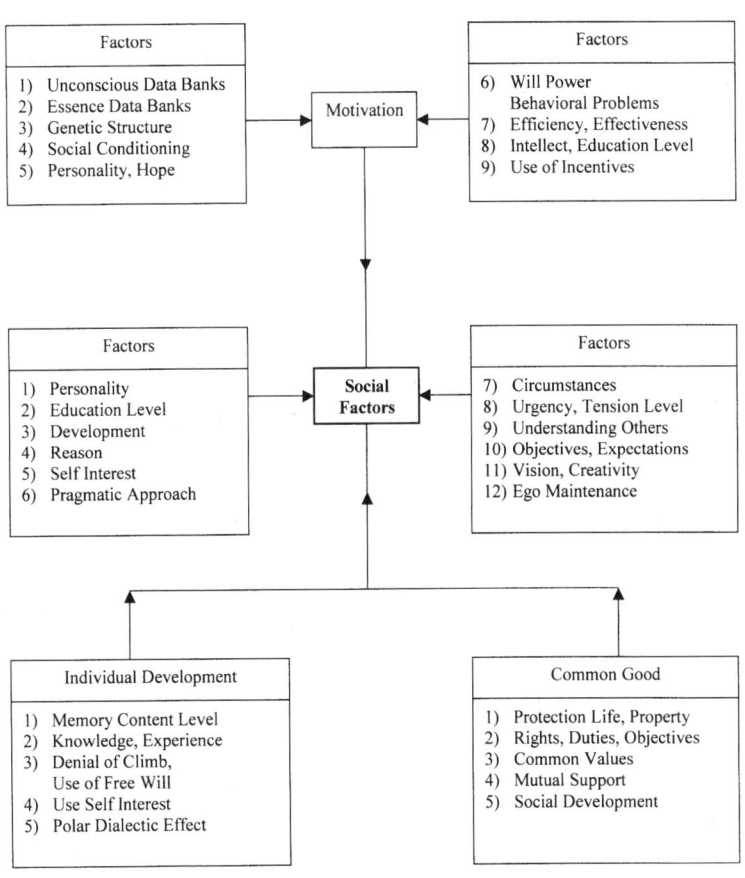

Figure19: Social Factors

this can become a strongly held unconscious expectation which influences other mind factors, e.g. Teenage students require the explanation of concepts at school that can take some minutes to cover, usually without scene changes. But the unconscious demand for a rapid scene change can generate a feeling of boredom, even with excellent teaching skills employed. It can even lead to a student looking at a friend and yawning, that in turn can have adverse effect on teacher motivation and lead to the use of relevant films instead. Here the films have a better chance of holding attention, because they use a fairly rapid scene change. In a group where the value given to learning is low, this effect can be very important in reducing the value of learning still further.

7. Another factor affecting social interaction is that in an egocentric market economy there is a marked tendency in society for individuals to regard each other with a negative bias, due to hard experience. This can be augmented by the conditioning effect during childhood to trust only family and school friends, due to sex related factors. These factors generate negative feelings that can be very important in personal relations and can lead to distrust, that is not merited. The like or dislike on first meeting someone can result largely from the perception responses to past unconscious conditioning. In this respect it is likely that the potential partner attraction for a marriage, relates significantly to the two sets of archetypes in the respective unconscious minds. Society usually sets the limits of conduct before sanctions are applied and then applies the sanctions but within these limits, individuals can usually choose their own path. If you decide to look after your own interests and attempt to get as much happiness as you can, even at the expense of others, this may appear attractive at the time. However, it can mean less real satisfaction because of going against Nature's re-

quirements, thus the resulting circumstances will not be supportive. Ego maintenance and enlargement can generate the urge for power, influence, respect and are prime motivating factors but they must support family interests and the common good of society or everyone is worse off. Thus the need to obtain the best balance of reason, emotion, feeling, desire, etc. with each factor contributing rationally to the whole.

8. Happiness, emotion, ethics, self-interest, reason and knowledge are all interrelated and should be considered as an integrated whole. Set out, by example, to provide a good social image, aim to be good at personal relations and be prepared to deal with the unexpected. What you do in society at present is usually considered less important, than your motive for doing it. Individual social growth requires increased knowledge of a more comprehensive kind with higher level concepts being necessary. Rapid scientific, technological and communication system development has occurred against a limited social system development, which includes reduction in spiritual and moral values, due to the decline of traditional Western religious influence and the rise of low level mass media conditioning. All these factors tend to operate in an egocentric, existential, materialistic and mass society, whose mass media values have at least equal influence with the education system in setting behavioral standards and life satisfaction levels. In turn, this has led to increased tension in individual, family and social life resulting in some 50 percent broken or high-tension homes. It is against this background that change has to take place, if Nature's requirements are to be met.

9. However, the political system cannot effect the necessary changes by setting out to increase the material standard of living plus crime prevention, so that the increased materialism can be enjoyed in peace. But these two factors at pres-

ent are the ones used by politicians wanting to maintain or gain political power and to measure success. A further factor in modern society is the reduction in the value and importance of higher feelings such as the aesthetic, deep emotion, love of beauty, etc. as forms of higher life, that we are all on the Life Mountain to effect. Another important factor affecting present society is the very limited social contact children have due to the threat of sex crime. Younger children are taken to and fetched from school and only speak to family and friends at home and others at school. This can lead to increased television watching and computer games, both of which do not provide any higher value concepts.

10. Any necessary change has to take into account the ability, motivation, education and training of those concerned with the correct attitude to life being very important, which itself requires an adequate background of relevant knowledge. Too many individuals today set out to maintain and enlarge the surface self, based on an inadequate background of knowledge of all life's possibilities in order to obtain the best way forward in the prevailing circumstances. In turn this requires consideration of the material, intellectual and spiritual aspects plus a rational self-interest supporting the family and society. In addition, the difference between the laws of science and mathematics and the social laws is that the social laws can be modified because humanity has been given certain freedom to do so, by using free will. However, certain of the social laws are independent of direct human control because they are innate in the data bank system content, e.g. ethics, with morality as free will modification.

11. If we respect what Nature requires and do not try to suppress conscience by the rationalized justification of self-interest, then we will be performing our duty to society. Experience can often determine the view taken and changes

in one social factor can affect others. Sometimes on the Life Mountain it may be necessary to rest for a while, in order to build up the resources to continue. Life on the Life Mountain is a learning process so it may be necessary to ask someone the way on occasions. Analyze your present level of satisfaction with life and compare it with what you consider is potentially available. Take into consideration that being in a materialistically comfortable situation, in an egocentric and existential mass society can generate inertia against change for improvement, with the necessary effort to achieve it not automatically following.

12. Necessary changes have to take place in a social situation where about 50 percent of the individuals live in broken or high-tension homes, where television viewing of soap operas is an escape from the actual problems of life, plus the public house, sports matches, etc. and production line employment to pay for it all. For many this is assumed to be the best that life can offer, so learn to live with it and obtain what happiness can be grasped. In an advanced market economy requiring a high material standard of living, production line type activity is essential but experience indicates that those with supporting social and cultural activities have the best production results, plus the least use of chemical stimulants by the workpeople. In addition, too old at 40 to be competitive in a market economy, has no place on the Life Mountain, where life is a developing process. This is Nature's requirement and Nature provides materialism in a market economy to enable the higher developmental levels to be achieved. Thus the market economy, egoism, individualism, will to power and influence, search for a higher standard of living, plus rational satisfaction of desires, all have their place in Nature' scheme of life, otherwise they would not exist, because Nature is Pure Logic. It is essential to retain the good things that have been developed in society

over the past ages, yet overcome the present limitations to adequate development in individual, family and social aspects. In this respect television has increased knowledge availability in certain areas such as travel, wild life, etc. but has never adequately tackled the social problems of the twenty-first century. The fundamental problem being how to achieve the best balance between materialism and individual life achievement, which also includes the intellectual and the spiritual.

13. In most cases the present problems in society have been building up over the last 50 years, due to the lack of a philosophy of life achievement. Thus the present type of life has been taken for granted as the only one available. In order that the necessary changes can be implemented, the electorate and the politicians need to realize the necessity of change, how to effect it and the advantages of so doing. All future changes must provide an adequate standard of material living, be based on the necessary knowledge and resources, plus the necessary drive to ensure that the inevitable obstacles are overcome. In addition, the value of success in climbing up the Life Mountain, as a value in its own right and established from an early age. Both technological and social development need to support the climb up the Life Mountain, which takes place in a climate of continual change. This will require an effective balance between the need for specialization and a more comprehensive overall view, that includes human development. In this respect it is essential to provide a higher standard of life achievement, rather than just a higher standard of material life. The introduction of a new philosophy of life will require the support of the present social system and its associated political patterns, in order to lift-off from its present plateau of performance. This will require the generation of the will to

improve by at least a significant majority of those concerned.

14. The selection of the best approach to living on the Life Mountain should take into account that thinking and decision making processes can be affected by data bank content at birth, with its subsequent modification by social conditioning. These influences can define the level of creative vision, including the drive to achieve self realization. In addition, the surface self is constantly changing and generating patterns that can support or hinder both social assessment of change and decisions about its future development. In addition, these factors can affect any desire to develop by climbing up and above the material level into the higher satisfaction level, with its increased level of life achievement. In this respect every individual is different and has different requirements, thus any development has to be rational self-development that meets the requirements of the family and society. In order to improve understanding of social aspects , it is helpful to have an indication of the relation between the Life Mountain and Reality, which is covered in Chapter 9 and Figure 20.

9

The Life Mountain and Reality

1. In order to understand the social factors and life achievement on the Life Mountain during the lifespan, an eight dimensional analysis of Reality can provide a helpful framework. But any model used will be attempting to penetrate the unknown and has to be based on recorded experience limited to the last 5,000 years. Eight dimensions have been used because it appears to give the best fit but that is no guarantee of accuracy. But as St. Augustine pointed out so forcefully, if concrete scientific evidence must be available before anything in the higher dimensions could be considered, then humanity had no possibility of development and progress. One important aspect of an analysis of Reality is how much it can help in the practical aspect of achieving a higher life achievement for all. This requires knowledge of how the eight dimensions affect human life.

2. The highest dimension is the Eighth as Ultimate Reality, as Absolute Spirit, that is beyond description in any national language. The intuitive mind, that is in the Upper Fourth Dimension can think abstractly of, but never about, the Absolute Spirit. However, if the intuitive mind develops eventually to reach the Fifth Dimension level, it may by using the Fundamental Language of that Dimension, be able to give at least some form of description of the Absolute Spirit. The Fifth, Sixth, and Seventh Dimensions use the

Fundamental Language, whilst the Fourth and Third Dimensions use national languages that are derived from the Fundamental Language as mind forms. These permit writing and speech, which is essential for social activity and knowledge.

3. The Seventh Dimension is one of pure and perfect intelligence and is the limit of description in national language. Whether the Seventh Dimension is part of the Eighth Dimension or separate is beyond human comprehension. In order to remain perfectly active the Seventh Dimension generates a perfect challenge to itself by creating six subordinate, hierarchical Dimensions, the activity of which provide the perfect challenge. The delegation to subordinate Dimensions is necessary because being Pure and Perfect, the Seventh Dimension is unable to participate in any imperfect activity. The Seventh Dimension created the Sixth Dimension with two levels as Upper and Lower. The Upper Sixth Dimension has Pure and Perfect intelligence that permits direct contact with the Seventh Dimension. The Lower Sixth Dimension was created by the Seventh Dimension in an imperfect Form to provide the most effective challenge to its Pure and Perfect intelligence. The Seventh Dimension then delegates to the Upper Sixth Dimension the task of bringing the Lower Sixth Dimension up to the Pure and Perfect level of the Upper Sixth Dimension in infinite time. In order for this to be achieved the Seventh Dimension then creates the Fifth, Fourth, Third, Second, First Dimensions. The Upper Fourth Dimension is the highest human level as the intuitive mind, with the Lower Fourth Dimension as the higher rational mind, which activates output from the intuitive mind, to enable development of intelligence on the Life Mountain.

4. The Upper Sixth Dimension contributes in three ways to this intelligence development. First, it provides the intuitive mind, the higher and lower rational minds and the

lust realization mind with suitable types of intelligence for their effective operation. Secondly, it provides the necessary factors to enable the deep self to input the intuitive mind with revelation, conscience, the urge to climb up the Life Mountain, deep satisfaction when appropriate, and the urge to obtain spiritual realization. Thirdly, it defines the next generation intelligence forms by providing the birth content and intensity of the higher and lower data banks and the essence data bank. The other aspect contributing to intelligence development on the Life Mountain is that the social conditioning and the data bank drives form a circular interaction, as already covered in Chapter 4 and Figure 15.

5. Consolidating and adding to Chapter 4 and Figure 15, the conscious mind generates social activity that conditions the innate data bank content. But the innate data bank content provides the unconscious drives into the conscious mind that determines the conscious mind activity. Thus the social conditioning and the innate data bank drives form a circular interaction. In turn, this has the potential to generate dialectic development of both the social system and the data bank content, as long as the revelation inputs from the deep self into the intuitive mind can be received and activated by the higher rational mind. This enables the data bank content to increase in depth and value and the social system to improve its performance in terms of institutional and social activity, thus enabling the total intelligence system to develop in the longer term.

6. To effect the necessary changes in intelligence factors on the Life Mountain the intensity of the innate data bank content can vary during the lifespan due to social conditioning, essence data bank inputs and mind evaluation system inputs. The essence data bank and the mind evaluation system activate each data bank at the required stage of development of the individual. The data banks of each individual

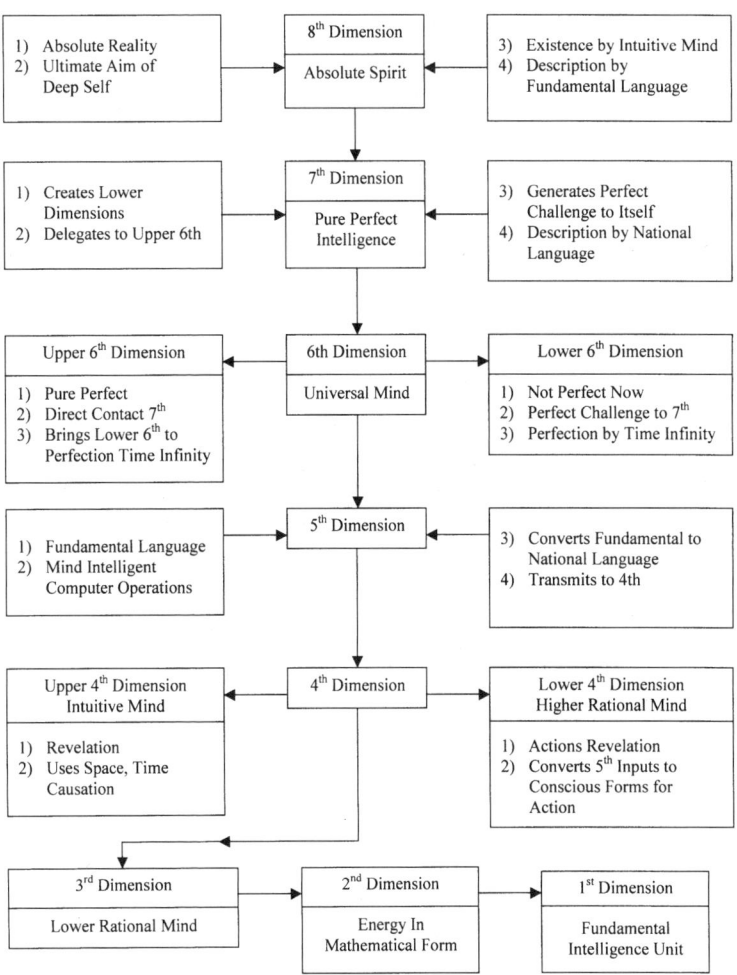

Figure 20: Life Mountain and Reality

have a hierarchical order determined by the essence data bank and the mind evaluation system. The essence data bank content for the lifespan is set at birth by the Upper Sixth Dimension and the essence data bank is not subjected to social conditioning. The essence data bank content of all individuals forms an integrated whole, set by the Upper Sixth Dimension, as does the summation of the content of all innate data banks. Once the content of the unconscious memory has been set at birth by the Upper Sixth Dimension, the unconscious memory receives and records all data bank changes during the lifespan. At the end of the lifespan the final unconscious memory content instantaneously enters the Lower Sixth Dimension to contribute to its development. Individual death is necessary because the Upper Sixth Dimension has to energize different unconscious memory and data bank system content, including the essence data bank for the next stage of the development of the Lower Sixth Dimension process. This will in infinite time enable the Lower Sixth Dimension to achieve the level of the Higher Sixth Dimension and then both parts of the Sixth Dimension will return into the Seventh Dimension. The individual self will then be able to comprehend the Eighth Dimension as Absolute Spirit and thus achieve the final aim of all life. Whether the unconscious memory patterns when they return into the Lower Sixth Dimension are given modified patterns by the Upper Sixth Dimension and then move to new bodies is not within human comprehension. However, this could provide an explanation of why dream content extends beyond living memory content.

7. The Seventh, Sixth, Fifth Dimensions use continuous time so there is no space or causation. The Fourth and Third Dimensions use infinitesimal interval time (clock time) operating in space, thus permitting causation. Space, time and causation enable social activity which enables intelligence

to develop itself over time. This is why the mind categories of space, time and causation have being in the Fourth and Third Dimensions. Free will gives a limited freedom of action with the other aspects being determined by inputs from the Fifth and Upper Sixth Dimensions. Life satisfaction and happiness provides the incentives for the development of intellectual and social systems. Thus happiness generating objective forms of satisfaction is a means to obtain self realization in order to provide development of the total system over time. The First Dimension is the fundamental intelligence unit that eventually develops into mathematical forms of energy and mind as the Second Dimension. Matter has no fundamental reality being energy organised in various mathematical forms. It could be possible that each element is a particular energy equation derived from an Absolute Virtual Equation. This could then appear when passed into perception and the mind evaluation system as the various chemical elements. Life achievement is covered in Chapter 10 and Figures 21/22.

10
Life Achievement

Ethics, Morality and Value

1. In making an assessment of life achievement, it is necessary to have adequate knowledge of the relation of ethics, morality and value and for all individuals to have a common understanding of the meaning of these three terms. Ethical principles are objective, universal, innate and unchanging. On the other hand morality is a social factor of judgment and depends on the particular society and the stage of its development. Thus moral principles are not innate, universal or have objective value. However, morality is usually based on ethical principles but ethical principles infringement is not usually punished by society, unless they are included in their morality. Infringement of ethical principles causes conscience, which if ignored, in the longer term, generates lack of satisfaction with life. Rational application of desires to meet Nature's requirements is ethical. Both ethics and morality are based on the polar of good and evil, but the problem today, is to obtain a universal definition of the terms good and evil. This in turn affects the definition of value, which can be directly connected to ego maintenance as a subjective entity.

2. The following is an actual example relating to parental pressure effect on ethics, morality and value. A very beautiful and talented, 22-year-old graduate, who had been

brought up very strictly with a high parental pressure to succeed, was considering her future. She had been given so much advice by her parents about working hard and climbing up the Life Mountain, that she decided to take a complete break from them. She decided to slide down the Life Mountain for a change and investigate what it was like, because it could not be worse than her past life. By the age of 26, she had had three partners, all married with young children in their marriage. By the end of the third relation she had become very bitter with life, yet still beautiful and talented. Her view was that men just did not have any moral standards any longer and she would have nothing more to do with them.

3. But soon the essence data bank content pressures for a happy family life became pressing, so she moved employment and location and set out to climb up the Life Mountain, which she did. She was, although still bitter with life, a much wiser person, who had come to realize that the individual can never take on Nature and win, by departing from the requirement to live by ethical standards. The three erring husbands returned to their wives and are still trying to give rational justification for their conduct, with limited success, because one of Nature's rules is that you cannot have your cake and eat it. The three erring husbands agreed that they had never seen such a beautiful and talented person so deeply unhappy with life, when they knew her. A very selfish life can appear very attractive at first but in the longer term one gets nothing but tears shed in the silence of solitude and many were until the climb commenced. Now happily married, it is interesting to speculate what she will tell her recent firstborn, when it is old enough to understand. It could be of help to her in deciding what to tell the firstborn if she considered the relationship of good, evil, value, morality, ethics, rational individual claims, family and social re-

quirements In ancient mythology Druj as the world's evil spirit was asked by the Goddess of Logic to justify being pure evil. Druj explained that without evil there could be no good and without good and evil humanity would not be able to have disputes, quarrels and immorality and they would become bored with life. Thus by generating evil, I serve a useful purpose. But if I go near the Summit of the Life Mountain the heat of its ethical purity gives me a conscience but elsewhere the lust, evil, hate, fear and craving after the unobtainable, makes my life's work have real meaning for me.

Motivation on the Life Mountain

1. In order to improve individual, family and social activity, it is necessary to consider the motivating drives affecting the individual, the family, social and work groups, with these four factors best considered as an integrated whole. The first requirement is to ensure that the motivation is both efficient and effective. For example, if a family member is meeting all self aims but these self aims do not meet family aims, then that individual is acting efficiently but not effectively. Thus the requirement for family members to be both efficient and effective in terms of aims. This requires the use of a rational self-interest supporting the family and the common good of society. This is an essential requirement for a modern progressive society. Individuals have different value systems, intellectual and education levels, experience and habits, thus incentives can have varying effects. Once a financial incentive has become the norm, it tends to lose its incentive value, which in the family can mean pocket money increases at intervals, without increas-

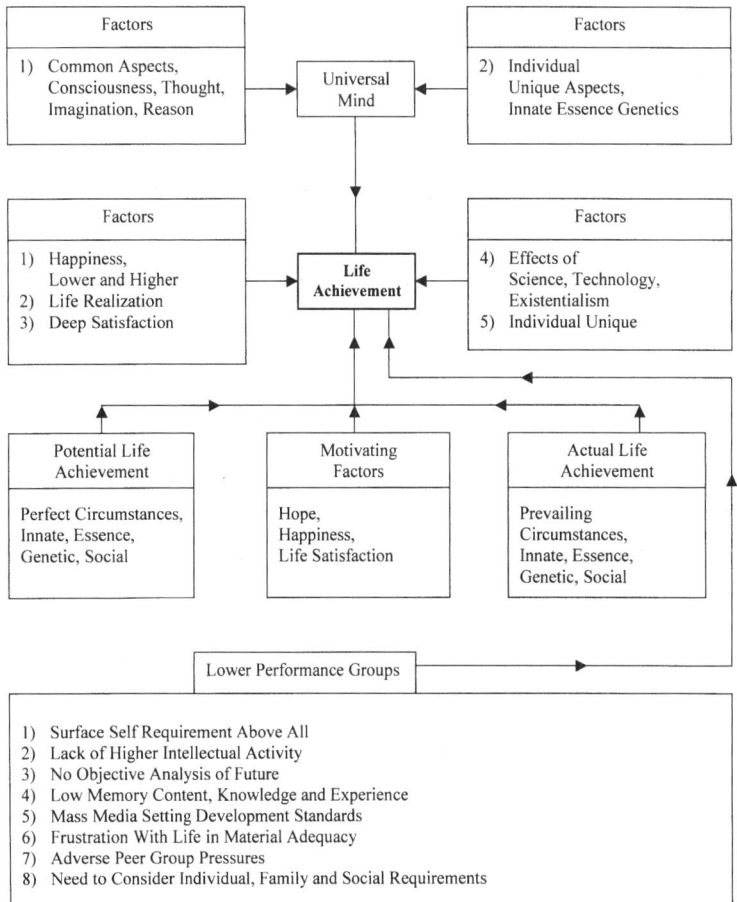

Figure 21: Life Achievement

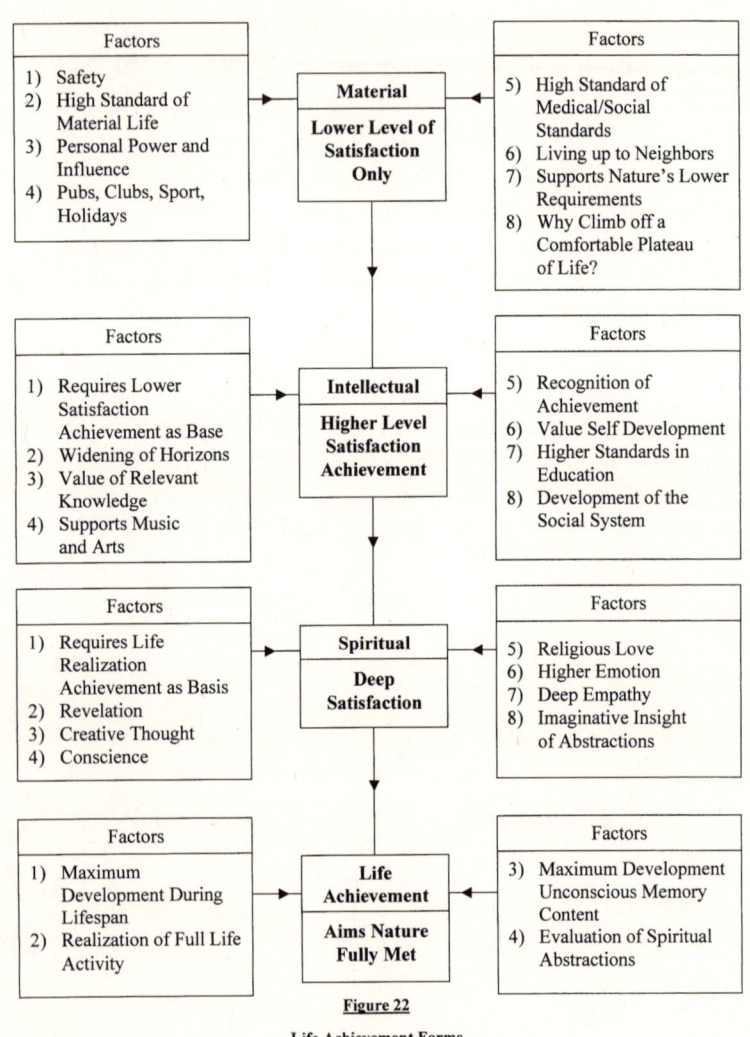

Figure 22

Life Achievement Forms

ing productivity in terms of work about the house and/or garden.

2. Individual motivation is affected by the innate data bank content, the essence data bank content and the genetic structure with all three operating continuously, whilest social conditioning, personality characteristics and circumstances operate over variable time factors. Thus it is possible for personality development to be above, the same or below the level of essence development, at a particular time in the lifespan. If personality development during the pre-teenage period has been considerably greater than the essence development this can lead to teenage behavioral problems and the urge to break free from parental influence in early teenage. In addition, it can lead to an unwillingness to follow traditional education and behavioral practices in school. This is the effect of the mind evaluation system, which is intelligent, attempting to force the conscious mind to correct the imbalance of personality and essence.

3. The following actual story about three neighbors illustrates some of these aspects. Peter, the retired owner of the center house, was working in his front garden when he was subjected to a very loud command, 'Peter, come here I want to talk to you.' Peter looked for the source of the command and found it as the head of the rising four-year-old daughter peering over the low wall separating next door. Peter who had been brought up in the early 1930s when a child was seen but not heard, stood his ground and went on gardening. The voice of command then carried by two small feet moved up onto the sidewalk of the road above and then descended into Peter's garden and was about to give Peter a severe dressing-down for disobedience to her command, when Mother rushed in from next door, took her daughter by the hand and scolded her for going onto the sidewalk alone. Peter's neighbor from the other side, who had wit-

nessed the pattern of events said, 'The generation gap was just as strong in the third century BCE when Plato wrote *The Republic* as a counter to it and a good laugh was had by all. The young girl had attended an advanced play school and had been given additional instruction on life's competitive aspects by her parents, using a light rein. All these factors had resulted in personality development greater than essence development. While such an approach has many advantages in terms of preparation for success in a market economy, disadvantages in terms of family and social relations can result, e.g. fitting in with peer groups and breaking away from parental control. In addition, there can be parental ego maintenance factors operating. Thus the need for parents to have sufficient psychological and sociological knowledge to ensure the best for the child, themselves and society and thus meet Nature's requirements.

Human Relations on the Life Mountain

1. Life achievement depends on human relations, because the individual without society has little real meaning. Human relations result from interaction of individuals with different personalities, value systems, self-interest, obligations, expectations, views, habits, hopes, vision, creativity, intelligence, education, ability, stress levels, problem solving ability, types of activity, social conditioning and ego maintenance. Thus an analysis of human relations is best effected using a pragmatic approach, which means that if the analysis appears to account for the results then use it, because no logical or scientific approach is possible. This can mean an assessment of the personalities and relevant experience of the individuals concerned, the use of personal experience that can on occasions lead to biased thinking, the

environmental influences, circumstances plus the social conditioning influences operating, including the mass media, where soap operas can come to have an apparent reality greater than ordinary life. Adding to the content covered on page 55 of chapter 4, in soap operas individuals are conditioned to identify with a multi-character situation in which inter-personal relations are usually aggressive on both sides. Viewers become locked onto a multi-character situation, all with varying sets of problems identified with the characters, which have been integrated by the script writers to generate viewer numbers, rather than being concerned with problem solving considerations. In addition, the viewer has no responsibility for problem outcomes, as in real life. Thus soap operas cannot be used as a background guide to human relations factors.

2. An important aspect in human relations is peer group pressures to conform to certain codes and standards of behavior, that can have a direct influence on the level and scope of inter-personal relations, especially if individuals come from groups with different value systems. If two individuals come from the same group, the subjects covered in discussion tend to be within group values. Peer group pressures to conform in a large, low development level group can make it impossible for that group to lift-off from a plateau of low level life satisfaction due to ignorance of any better alternative. It can also prevent individuals and small groups from attempting to climb up the Life Mountain. In addition, groups with strong religious aspects supported by a political philosophy ensure that self realization follows defined patterns. On the other hand, in an existential philosophy group where individuals set out to build up their self by their own efforts, this can reduce the social aspect in development.

3. In human relations the Universal Mind ensures that

all individuals have some common mind aspects such as consciousness and thought, plus the ability to understand, imagine and reason. On the other hand, each individual is given certain factors that are unique to that individual. Thus each individual is different from all the others in some aspects, with each human life having a unique value and the capacity to contribute uniquely to the whole society. By maximizing their contribution each individual gains the maximum self realization and thus life achievement. The individual's unique qualities are in the unconscious innate data bank content, the essence data bank content and the genetic coding content. During the lifespan social conditioning ensures that the unconscious data bank content of the individual is modified in a variety of ways, in order that intellectual development can take place. All these factors coupled with the polar dialectic form of Life Mountain operation, the five levels of mind, plus the use of the motivating forms of hope, expectations, happiness, life satisfaction, deep satisfaction and life achievement ensure that the Life Mountain is a developing entity with the final aim of perfection at time infinity.

Individual Development on the Life Mountain

1. Individual development is directly connected to life achievement, with five social group types determining individual potential development. The first group type is where individuals cannot reach their material Sufficiency Level due to genetic limitations, poverty, etc. These individuals should aim to reach their maximum feasible rational potential. In the second group type the individuals have insufficient memory content to stimulate the other mind factors into progressive activity. Thus they are unable to think

higher than the material level advantages of life and in thinking this, they are convinced that they are correct, because there is no mind evaluation system to give a higher level thinking process Some individuals in this group may reach their material Sufficiency Level but the majority are unlikely to attain that level of materialism. Individuals in this group will attain various levels of lower level happiness. In the third group type the individuals have the ability and capacity to reach their material Sufficiency Level of development but lack the motivation to do so, because they are content to stay where they are, achieving some level of lower level happiness. This group is complex because of the effects of mass media conditioning and the use of chemical stimulants by some members. In the fourth group type individuals upon reaching their material Sufficiency Level decide to mix making the climb with lust achievement, in an attempt to have their cake and eat it. As this is against Nature's requirements, this approach will fail in the longer term. In the fifth group type individuals upon reaching their material Sufficiency Level decide to climb up the Life Mountain using free will and a rational self interest supporting the family and the common good of society. These individuals will be supporting their innate urge to climb up the Life Mountain triggered by reaching their Sufficiency Level. These individuals have the potential of achieving higher level happiness with the possibility of deep satisfaction. This group should be used as an example for the other groups.

2. The following story illustrates some of these group types. Deep inside a mountain a group of individuals had spent their whole lives in a cave illuminated by a flickering fire. One day one of the members had an urge to explore some tunnels, which he did and eventually came out into sunlight and open beautiful countryside. At first, the light

intensity blinded him, but he was eventually able to see the great beauty of the outside world because his innate data bank system had been activated by it. He then started to return to his group to tell them of his discovery but realized on the way, that he had no conceptual language, by which he could tell them. On return to his group he persuaded another member to go with him to explore the tunnels. He then showed that member the glory of the outside world. He then repeated the process until the whole group were in the sunlight. Their first task was then to develop a conceptual language by which they could communicate and thus be able to make a comparison of the two forms of life. They had the choice of climbing up the Life Mountain in the new world of change or returning to the cave fire, that had given some mental security because it did not change but only flickered and the pressures of life were minimal. However, the cave location does not meet Nature's requirement for humanity to develop to perfection by time infinity, so that form of life can have no long term meaning and value. But until they had moved from the cave into the light they could never know that. Thus the importance of knowledge of the Life Mountain activities in decision making and life achievement. In addition, the need of effort and determination to overcome any problems that stand in the way. In achieving the maximum development level available, individuals will then be maximizing their contribution to the achievement of Nature's aims. If one restricts one's life aims to the lower level subjective happiness as material form as the best life that is available then one must live an unrealized life, unless corrective action is taken.

Planning for Increased Life Satisfaction

1. The first requirement for improving low level life achievement and satisfaction is for politicians to make themselves fully aware of how the quality of life can be improved, whilst still maintaining a high standard of living in an advanced market economy, that itself has to operate in a competitive world economy. This will include intellectual and personality development, the widening of horizons, high aesthetic and ethical standards with all these factors considered in terms of the material, intellectual and spiritual. In order to achieve this, it will be necessary for the education system to give the correct priority to human development and life achievement, whilst integrating the examination system to ensure an efficient market economy. This follows, because the total resources available for human development depend on the economic system being efficient. But at present, parental pressures for the education system to concentrate on providing their teenagers with the required grades in examinations, has resulted in life quality aspects having too low a priority. As a result the mass media including soap operas and low-grade films now have too much influence in determining life quality. In turn, this forces social affairs departments with their limited resources, to concentrate on solving the resulting social problems and thus they have insufficient resources left to provide for the necessary individual and social development aspects, so necessary to reducing the present social problems. Thus the situation is circular with individual development and life achievement the way to break out of it. In the future, these two factors will be essential to an efficient market economy, with its requirement for social harmony and cohesion, Thus the requirement for Higher

Education to provide a philosophy of economic and social development.

2. The necessary changes will require a change in social values from the present type, to ones in which real value is given to self realization, learning and the higher forms of life achievement. As life is a learning process the experience of others can be valuable as long as it is not from low performance groups, that are locked onto a low level performance plateau on the Life Mountain. Any changes required should be effected by self-help within potential to avoid stress. Assess your situation in terms of knowledge, truth, value and responsibility remembering that power, influence and respect are powerful motivating factors. Take into account education, training, values, attitude to life and motivation. Individuals should be able to say that during their lifespan they had made full use of their potential and that they had overcome challenges and problems in such a way that they had enjoyed their life. They had lived by setting out during their life to make the best use of the potential that they had been born with, when circumstances were taken into account. This is what Nature requires and supports in terms of rational self-interest, support of the family and the common good of society. Life, when taken over the lifespan can be enjoyable and stimulating, as long as the basic forces in life are understood and the appropriate self realization achieved. It is necessary that society takes full advantage of a rapidly advancing science, technology and communication systems and not become adversely affected by it. This will enable individuals to have a deeper level of life satisfaction and achievement.

3. This book has covered the objective general principles of life as an individual and as a member of society. It is advisable to read the whole book through again and look for examples in your own life and in the society around you.

Then adapt these general principles to the situation and circumstances in your own life in society, in order to help others and increase your life satisfaction and life achievement.

Appendix A

184 Chief Thinkers Providing Background Data

Chief Thinkers BCE

Thales	6th	Anaxagoras	5th	Liezi	3rd
Anaximander	6th	Protagoras	5th	Epicurus	3rd
Mahavira	6th	Badarayana	5th	Stoics	3rd
The Buddha	6th	Leucippus	5th	Master Lu	3rd
Xenophanes	6th	Democritus	5th	Han Fei	3rd
Pythagoras	6th	Antisthenes	5th	Zhongshu	2nd
Heraclitus	5th	Socrates	5th	Patanjali	2nd
Confucius	5th	Mozi	5th	Lucretius	1st
Lao Tzu	5th	Plato	4th	Cicero	1st
Parmenides	5th	Aristotle	4th	Virgil	1st
Zengzi	5th	Zhuangzi	4th	Ovid	1st
Empedocles	5th	Mencius	4th		

Chief Thinkers CE

Philo	1st	Al Farabi	10th	Madhva	13th
Ptolemy	1st	Avicenna	11th	St Aquinas	13th
Nagarjuna	2nd	Zhang Zai	11th	Beneventuri	13th
Plotinus	3rd	Cheng Hao	11th	R Bacon	13th
Guo Xiang	3rd	Ramanuja	11th	Duns Scotus	13th
Vasubandhu	4th	Anselm	11th	Dante	13th
St. Augustine	4th	Al Ghazali	11th	Ockham	14th
Ishvarakrishna	5th	Abelard	12th	Marsilius	14th
Muhammad	7th	Averroes	12th	Petrarch	14th
Guadapada	8th	Zhu Xi	12th	Kempis	14th
Sankara	9th	Ibn Arabi	13th	Machiavelli	15th
Al Kindi	9th	Grosseteste	13th	Yangming	15th

Chief Thinkers CE

More	16th	Newton	17th	Schelling	19th		
Erasmus	16th	Leibniz	17th	Hegel	19th		
Copernicus	16th	Berkeley	18th	Schopenhauer	19th		
Luther	16th	Montesquieu	18th	Comte	19th		
Calvin	16th	Wesley	18th	Stirner	19th		
F Bacon	16th	Voltaire	18th	Tocqueville	19th		
Kelper	17th	Hume	18th	Kierkegaard	19th		
Galileo	17th	Rousseau	18th	Feuerbach	19th		
Descartes	17th	Dai Zhen	18th	Cournot	19th		
Geulincx	17th	Burke	18th	JS Mill	19th		
Pascal	17th	Adam Smith	18th	Proudhon	19th		
Adhvarin	17th	Kant	18th	Marx	19th		
Spinoza	17th	Goethe	18th	Bakunin	19th		
Hobbes	17th	Fichte	18th	Arnold	19th		
Burthogge	17th	St Simon	19th	Fustel	19th		
Boyle	17th	Godwin	19th	Darwin	19th		
Locke	17th	Bentham	19th	Spencer	19th		
Malebranche	17th	Coleridge	19th	Green	19th		

Chief Thinkers CE

Dilthey	19th	Bloomfield	20th	Barthes	20th
Pierce	19th	Lenin	20th	Russell	20th
Saussure	19th	Alexander	20th	Lacan	20th
Brentano	19th	Dewey	20th	Morris	20th
Nietzche	19th	Freud	20th	Sebeck	20th
Czanne	19th	Scheler	20th	Vodica	20th
James	19th	Croce	20th	Eco	20th
Sorel	19th	Gandhi	20th	Mukarovsky	20th
Bosanquet	19th	Baker	20th	Jakobson	20th
Bradley	19th	Backelaard	20th	Halliday	20th
Kropotkin	19th	Wittgenstein	20th	Levi-Strauss	20th
Durkheim	19th	Jung	20th	Chomsky	20th
Weber	19th	Hjelmsleu	20th	Sartre	20th
Mach	20th	Mao Tse-Tung	20th	Lobman	20th
Hobhouse	20th	Godamer	20th	Piaget	20th
Bergson	20th	Fung Yu-Lan	20th	Ayer	20th
Husseri	20th	Heidegger	20th	Scanlon	20th
Einstein	20th	Merleau	20th	Searle	20th
Franks	20th	Adorno	20th	Ouspensky	20th
Moscow Circle	20th	Althusser	20th		

Background Religious Aspects

Magic	Zarathustra	Shinto
Animism	Buddhism	Sikhism
Totem	Jainism	African
Hinduism	Confucius	Quakerism
Judaism	Tao	Anglican
Minoan	Christianity	Mormon
Babylon	Gnosticism	Jehovah's Witness
Egypt	Islam	7-day Adventist
Ancient Greece	Sufism	Christian Science

Appendix B

Philosophical Aspects

- Aesthetics
- A Posteriori
- A Priori
- Alienation
- Anarchism
- Categories
- Causation
- Change
- Concepts/ideas
- Conservatism
- Cynicism
- Determinism
- Dialectic
- Dictatorship
- Dualism
- Education
- Empiricism
- Epistemology
- Essence
- Existentialism
- Fabianism
- Freedom
- Humanism
- Individualism
- Inferences
- Knowledge
- Language
- Law
- Liberalism
- Logical Empiricism
- Materialism
- Metaphysics
- Morality
- Self-development
- Nationalism
- National Socialism
- Naturalism
- Nihilism
- Nominalism
- Occasionalism
- Pantheism
- Paradigm
- Phenomenology
- Pluralism
- Positivism
- Post Modernism
- Pragmatism
- Rationalism
- Reason
- Realism
- Reality
- Rep. Gov.
- Socialism
- Social Systems
- Scepticism
- State
- Structuralism
- Substance
- Truth
- Universals

Mind Aspects

- Conscious
- Unconscious
- Innate Factors
- Cognitive Systems
- Memory
- Understanding
- Imagination
- Will
- Perception
- Ego
- Self
- Emotions
- Passions
- Intuition
- Soul
- Use of Language
- Mental Monism
- Physical Monism
- Occasionalism
- Interactionism
- Identify Theory
- Dualism
- Materialism
- Nerve Realism

High Energy Aspects

History Atomic Theory	Quantum Theory	Forces in Atoms
Space-Time	Molecular Structures	Atomic Orbits
Special Relativity	Atomic Particles	Atomic/Chemical Processes

Bibliography

Religious Aspects

Albert the Great, *On Union with God* (Continuum, 2000)
Ariel, D., *What Do Jews Believe?* (Reider, 1988)
Bowden, H., *Ancient Civilizations* (Times Books, 1998)
Bowker, J., *Oxford Dictionary of World Religions* (Oxford University Press, 1997)
Bucaille, M., *The Bible, the Koran and Science* (TAJ, 1993)
Carlson, R., *Handbook of the Soul* (Piatkus, 1996)
Chittick, W.C., *The Self Disclosure of God, Al Arabi* (State University New York, 1997)
Cohn-Sherbok, D., *A Concise Encyclopaedia of Judaism* (One World Oxford, 1998)
Dawood, N.I., *Koran* (Penguin, 1997)
Drosnin, M., *Dead Sea Scrolls* (HarperCollins, 1996)
Drosnin, M., *The Bible Code* (Weidenfield and Nicolson, 1997)
Ellingworth, P., *Good News Study Bible* (Weidenfeld and Nicolson, 1997)
Elon, A., *Jerusalem* (Kodansha America, 1995)
Giolitto, V., *The Upanishads* (Continuum, 2000)
Gordon, C., *The Bible and the Ancient Near East* (Norton, 1995)
Green, V., *A New History of Christianity* (Sutton, 1996)
Grierson, R., *Ark of the Covenant* (Weidenfield and Nicolson, 1999)
Hope, J., *Introducing Buddhism* (Icon Books, 1997)
Humphrey, N., *Soul Searching* (Chatto and Windus, 1991)
Johnson, G., *Fire in the Mind. Science, Faith and the Search for Order* (Viking, 1995)
Kemp, A., *Practical Paganism* (Robert Hale, 1999)

Mabrouk, L., *Soul's Journey after Death* (Daral-Taqua, 1994)
Metzger, B.M., *Oxford Companion to the Bible* (Oxford University Press, 1997)
Nicholson, R.A., *The Mystics of Islam* (Arkana, 1989)
Parker, T.H., *Calvinism* (Geoffrey Chapman, 1995)
Rogerson, J., *The Oxford Illustrated History of the Bible* (Oxford University Press, 2001)
Smart, N., *Atlas of World Religions* (Oxford University Press, 1999)
Sumedho, A., *The Mind and the Way, Buddhist Reflections on Life* (Reider, 1995)
Thomas, K., *Religion and the Decline of Magic* (Weidenfeld and Nicolson, 1997)
Tobin, G., *The Wisdom of St. Patrick* (Ballantine, 1999)
Turner, A.K., *The History of Hell* (Robert Hale, 1998)
Vardey, I., *God in All Worlds* (Pantheon, 1995)
Walvin, J., *The Quakers* (John Murray, 1997)
Wilson, A., *World Scripture* (Paragon House, 1995)
Wilson, A.N., *Paul, The Mind of the Apostle* (Sinclair Stevenson, 1997)
Wise, M., *Dead Sea Scrolls* (HarperCollins, 1996)

Mythology

Attar, F., *Conference of the Birds* (Continuum, 2000)
Bailey, A., *The Caves of the Sun, Origin Mythology* (Johnathan Cape, 1997)
Calk, C., *Mysteries of the Unexplained* (Readers Digest, 1982)
Dixon-Kennedy, M., *North American Myths* (Blandford, 1996)
Grant, M., *Who's Who in Classical Mythology* (Routledge, 1999)
Jones, A., *Dictionary of World Folklore* (Larousse, 1995)
Jones, D.M., *The Mythology of the Americas* (Lorenz Books, 2001)
MacGregor-Athers, S.L., *Concealed Mysteries* (Continuum, 2000)
March, J., *Dictionary of Classical Mythology* (Cassell, 1998)
Radford, E., *The Encyclopaedia of Superstitions* (Helicon, 1995)
Scott-Littleton, C., *Mythology* (Duncan Baird, 2002)

Sykes, E., *Neo-Classical Mythology* (Routledge, 2002)
Willis, R., *World Mythology* (Duncan Baird, 1993)

Science and Technology

Atkins, P., *The Periodic Kingdom* (Weidenfeld and Nicolson, 1995)
Barnes-Surrney, R., *Science Desk Reference* (Macmillan USA, 1995)
Barrow D., *The Anthropic Cosmological Principle* (Oxford University Press, 1985)
Barrow, J.D., *Origin of the Universe* (Weidenfeld and Nicolson, 1996)
Carey, J., *Faber Book of Science* (Faber and Faber, 1995)
Dawkins, P., *River Out of Eden* (Weidenfeld and Nicolson, 1995)
Dawkins, R., *Climbing Mount Improbable* (Softback Preview, 1996)
Deutsch, D., *The Fabric of Reality* (Penguin, 1997)
Dyson, G., *Darwin among the Machines* (Allan Lane, 1997)
Feynman, R.P., *The Character of Physical Law* (Penguin, 1988)
Feynman, R.P., *The Strange Theory of Light and Matter* (Penguin, 1995)
Green, B., *The Elegant Universe* (Johnathan Cape, 1999)
Gribben, J., *Companion to the Cosmos* (Weidenfeld and Nicolson, 1994)
Gribben, J., *Science, a History 1543–2001* (BCA, 2002)
Gribben J., *Q is for Quantum, Particle Quantum Physics* (Weidenfeld and Nicolson, 1994)
Hawking, S., *A Brief History of Time* (BCA, 1998)
Hawking, S., *Nature of Space and Time* (Princeton University Press, 1996)
Hawking, S., *The Universe in a Nutshell* (Bantam Press, 2001)
Hellemans, A., *Timetables of Science* (Simon and Schuster, 1989)
Hey, T., *Einstein's Mirror* (Cambridge University Press, (1997)
Horgan, J., *The End of Science* (Little, Brown and Company, 1996)
Jones, S., *In the Blood* (HarperCollins, 1996)
Kaku, M., *Hyperspace* (Oxford University Press, 1994)
Kitcher, P., *The Lives to Come* (Penguin, 1996)

Klein, E., *Conversation with the Sphinx, Physics Paradoxes* (Souvenir, 1996)
Kolata, G., *Clone* (Penguin, 1997)
Krauss, L.M., *The Physics of Star Trek* (HarperCollins, 1996)
Leakey, R., *The Sixth Extinction* (Weidenfeld and Nicolson, 1998)
Levy, D. H., *Book of the Cosmos* (Macmillan, 2000)
Luck, S., *Science and Technology Encyclopaedia* Phillips, 1998)
Morris, R., *Achilles in the Quantum Universe* (Souvenir, 1994)
Murray, J., *Making the Modern World* (Science Museum, 1992)
Quammen, D., *The Song of the Dodo, Evolution* (Johnathan Cape, 1995)
Rees, M., *Just Six Numbers, Forces Shaping the Universe* (Weidenfeld and Nicolson, 1997)
Ridley, M., *A Darwin Selection* (Fontana, 1994)
Ridley, M., *Genome* (Fourth Estate, 1977)
Rose, S., *Lifelines Biology, Freedom and Determinism* (Penguin, 1997)
Russell, P., *The Awakening Earth, the Global Brain* (Arkana, 1988)
Schwartz, J., *Introducing Einstein* (Icon Books, 1999)
Silver, B.L., *The Ascent of Science* (Oxford University Press, 1998)
Stachel, J., *Einstein's Miraculous Year* (Princeton University Press, 1998)
Stewart, L., *Nature's Numbers* (Weidenfeld and Nicolson, 1995)
Strain, P., *Looking at Earth* (Turner Atlanta, 1996)
Tudge, T., *The Day Before Yesterday, Evolution* (Johnathan Cape, 1995)
Walker, A., *Wisdom of the Bones* (Weidenfeld and Nicolson, 1996)
Walker, P.M., *Dictionary of Science and Technology* (Larousse, 1995)
Watson, J.D., *A Passion for DNA* (Oxford University Press, 2000)
Watts, D.J., *Small Worlds* (Princeton University Press, 1995)
Williams, G., *Plan and Purpose in Nature* (Weidenfeld and Nicolson, 1996)
Wills, C., *Children of Prometheus* (Penguin, 1998)
Wynn, G.M., *Five Major Ideas of Science* (Little, Brown and Company, 1996)
Zimmer, C., *Evolution* (Heinemann, 2002)

General Information

Anderson, T., *The Chambers Encyclopaedia* (Chambers Harrap, 2001))

Beattie, A., *The New Kobbes Opera Book* (Ebury Press, 1997)

Boorstin, D.J., *The Discoverers* (Random House, 1983)

Burchfield, R.W., *Modern English Usage* (Oxford University Press, 1996)

Drabble, M., *Oxford Companion to Literature* (Oxford University Press, 1995)

Flavell, L., *Dictionary of Proverbs* (Kyle Cathie, 1997)

Fortey, R., *Life, An Unauthorized Biography* (HarperCollins, 1996)

Hemming, J., *Atlas of Exploration* (Phillips, 1996)

Hutchinson Softback Encyclopaedia (Softback Preview, 1996)

Jordan, P., *The Atlantis Syndrome* (Sutton Publishing, 2001)

Kennedy, M., *The Oxford Dictionary of English Music* (Oxford University Press, 1994)

Laclotte, M., *Treasures of the Louvre* (Artabras, 1998)

Latham, R., *Lucretius on the Nature of the Universe* (Penguin, 1994)

Leakey, R., *The Origins of Humankind* Weidenfeld and Nicolson, 1994)

Lee, M., *Book of Facts* (Chambers Harrap, 1996)

Munro, D., *Oxford Dictionary of the World* (Oxford University Press, 1995)

Orchard, C., *Royal Geographical Society Illustrated, Scriptum Edition* (RGS, 1997)

Osborne, H., *Oxford Companion to Art* (Oxford University Press, 1993)

Partington, A., *Oxford Dictionary of Quotations* (Oxford University Press, 1996)

Ricks, C., *Oxford Books of Verse* (Oxford University Press, 1992)

Sadie, S., *The Cambridge Music Guide* Cambridge University Press, 1995)

Speake, T., *Oxford Dictionary of Idioms* (Oxford University Press, 1998)

Tolkein, J.R.R., *The Lord of the Rings* (HarperCollins, 1998)

Waller, P., *Chronology of the 20th Century* (Helicon, 1995)

History

Bahn, P.G., *The Story of Archeology* (Weidenfeld and Nicolson, 1996)
Barraclough, C., *Times Atlas of World History* (Times Books, 1994)
Bartlett, R., *Medieval Panorama* (Thames and Hudson, 2001)
Becker, J., *The Chinese* (John Murrow, 2000)
Boardman, J., *The Oxford History of the Classical World* (Oxford University Press, 1986)
Cahill, T., *How the Irish Saved Civilization* (Hodder and Stoughton, 1975)
Cannon, J., *The Oxford Companion to British History* (Oxford University Press, 1997)
Daily Telegraph Concise World Atlas (Telegraph Publications, 1980)
Dersin, D., *Austro-Hungarian Empire 1848–1918* (Time-Life, 2000)
Dersin, D. *Byzantine Empire 330 CE–1453 CE* (Time-Life, 1998)
Dersin, D., *Celtic Ireland 400 CE–1200CE* (Time-Life, 1995)
Dersin, D., *Classical Athens* (Time-Life, 1997)
Dersin, D., *Egypt 3050 BCE–30 BCE* (Time-Life, 1997)
Dersin, D., *European Golden Age 1500–1575* (Time-Life, 1999)
Dersin, D., *Europe's Romantic Era* (Time-Life, 2000)
Dersin, D., *France Age of Reason 1660–1800* (Time-Life, 1999)
Dersin, D., *Imperial China 960 CE–1368 CE* (Time-Life, 1998)
Dersin, D., *Imperial Russia 1696–1917* (Time-Life, 1998)
Dersin, D., *Islamic World 570 CE–1445 CE* (Time-Life, 1999)
Dersin, D., *Japan 1000 CE1700 CE* (Time-Life, 1999)
Dersin, D., *Medieval Europe 800 CE–1500 CE* (Time-Life, 1997)
Dersin, D., *Renaissance Italy 1400 CE–1550 CE* (Time-Life, 1999)
Dersin, D., *Roman Empire 100 BCE–200 CE* (Time-Life, 1997)
Dersin, D., *Vikings 800 CE–1100 CE* (Time-Life, 1995)
Ebrey, P.B., *Cambridge Illustrated History China* (Cambridge University Press, 1997)

Fagan, B.H., *The Seventy Mysteries of the Ancient World* (Thames and Hudson, 2001)
Filder, A., *Alexander the Great* (Duncan Baird, 2001)
Freeman, G., *Egypt, Greece and Rome* (Oxford University Press, 1996)
Gascoigne, B., *The Great Moghuls* (Constable, 1998)
Gibbon, E., *The History of the Decline and Fall of the Roman Empire* (Penguin, 1996)
Grun, B., *The Timetables of History* (Simon and Schuster, 1991)
Harris, N., *History of Ancient Greece* (Hamlyn, 2000)
Harris, N., *History of Ancient Rome* (Hamlyn, 2000)
Haywood, J., *Encyclopaedia of the Viking Age* (Thames and Hudson, 2000)
Heath, D., *Introducing Romanticism* (Icon Books, 2000)
Katz, F., *The Ancient American Civilization* (Phoenix Books, 1988)
Kostof, S., *A History of Architecture* (Oxford University Press, 1991)
O'Brien, P.K., *Phillips Atlas of World History* (Phillips, 1999)
Quirke, D., *The British Museum Book on Ancient Egypt* (British Museum, 1996)
Rawlinson, G., *Herodotus Histories* (Quality, 1997)
Roberts, J.M., *Eastern Asia and Classical Greece* (Duncan Baird, 1996)
Roberts, J.M., *Emerging Powers in Europe* (Duncan Baird, 1998)
Roberts, J.M., *History of Europe* (Helicon, 1996)
Roberts, J.M., *History of the World* (Softback Preview, 1992)
Roberts, J.M. *Prehistory and the First Civilization* (Duncan Baird, 1998)
Roberts, J.M., *Rome and the Classical West* (Duncan Baird, 1998)
Roberts, J.M., *The Age of the Revolution in Europe* (Duncan Baird, 1995)
Roberts, J.M., *The European Empires* (Duncan Baird, 1998)
Roberts, J.M., *The Far East 500 CE–1000 CE* (Duncan Baird, 1998)
Roberts, J.M., *The Making of the European Age* (Duncan Baird, 1998)
Roberts, J.M., *The New Global Era* (Duncan Baird 1998)
Ross, J., *Cicero, The Nature of the Gods* (Penguin, 1977)
Saul, N., *Companion of the Medieval England* (Tempus, 2000)

Shaw, I., *The Oxford History of Ancient Egypt* (Oxford University Press, 2000)
Silverman, D.P., *Ancient Egypt* (Duncan Baird, 1997)
Sligmann, B., *History of Magic* (Pantheon, 1997)
Temple, R., *The Genius of China* (Prion, 1998)
The Times Illustrated History of Europe (Armesto, 1998)

Philosophy

Appignanesi, R., *Introducing Marx* (Icon Nooks, 1998)
Applebaum, D., *The Vision of Kant* (Element, 1991)
Ayer, A.J., *Language, Truth and Logic* (Penguin, 1991)
Ayer, A.J., *The Problem of Knowledge* (Penguin, 1990)
Berlinksi, D., *Calculus, The Philosophy of Mathematics* (Heinemann, 1996)
Blackburn, S., *Oxford Dictionary of Philosophy* (Oxford University Press, 1994)
Bosanquet, B., *Introducing Hegel's Aesthetics* (Penguin, 1993)
Bullock, A., *The New Fontana Dictionary of Modern Thought* (HarperCollins, 1999)
Cobley, P., *Introducing Semiotics* (Icon Books, 1998)
Collinson, D., *Fifty Eastern Thinkers* (Routledge, 2000)
Concise Routledge Encyclopaedia of Philosophy (Routledge, 2000)
Cranston, M., *Social Contract, Rousseau* (Penguin, 1968)
Crystal, D., *The Cambridge Encyclopaedia of Language* (Cambridge University Press, 1997)
De Bono, E., *Textbook of Wisdom* (Viking, 1996)
Evans, G.R., *Fifty Key Medieval Thinkers* (Routledge, 2002)
Fagles, R., *The Iliad, Homer* (Softback Preview, 1997)
Fagles, R., *The Odyssey, Homer* (Softback Preview, 1997)
Findlay, I.N., *Hegel's Philosophy of Mind* (Oxford University Press, 1971)
Fraser, J.G., *Illustrated Golden Bough* (Softback Preview, 1977)
Garratt, C., *Introducing Descartes* (Icon Books, 1998)
Garratt, G., *Introducing Romanticism* (Icon Books, 1999)

George, A., *The Epic of Gilgamesh* (Lane, 1999)
Gould, S.J., *Life's Grandeur* (Johnathan Cape, 1996)
Hampson, N., *The Enlightenment* (Penguin, 1982)
Hazel, J., *The Greek World* (Routledge, 2000)
Heath, D., *Introducing Romanticism* (Icon Books, 1999)
Hofstadter, D.R., *Godel, Escher, Bach* (Penguin, 1998)
Honderich, T., *Oxford Companion to Philosophy* (Oxford University Press, 1995)
Hood, S., *Introducing Sade* (Icon Books, 1995)
Howatson, M.D., *Oxford Companionship to Classics* (Oxford University Press, 1993)
Huxley, A., *Brave New World* (Flamingo, 1994)
Jertsen, D.G., *Science and Philosophy* (Penguin, 1994)
Jones, O.P., *An Intelligent Guide to the Classics* (Duckworth, 1999)
Joyce, J., *Ulysses* (Picador, 1997)
Korkos, A., *Introducing Camus* (Icon Books, 1995)
Kwok, M.H., *Tao Te Ching* (Element, 1993)
Lau, D., *Confucius, The Analects* (Penguin, 1979)
Lechte, J., *Fifty Contemporary Thinkers* (Routledge, 1994)
MacQuarrie, J., *Existentialism* (Penguin, 1972)
Marshall, P., *Anarchism* (Fantana Press, 1992)
McClelland, J.S., *History of Western Political Thought* (Routledge, 1996)
McGreal, I.P., *Great Thinkers of the Eastern World* (HarperCollins, 1995)
Mitchell, S., *Tao Te Ching* (Frances Lincoln, 1999)
Murdoch, I., *Metaphysics as a Guide to Morals* (Penguin, 1992)
Osborne, R., *Introducing Sociology* (Icon Books, 1996)
Petry, J., *Hegel Philosophy of Subjective Spirit Anthropology* (Reidel, 1979)
Petry, J., *Hegel Philosophy of Subjective Spirit Introduction* (Reidel, 1979)
Petry, J., *Hegel Philosophy of Subjective Spirit Phenomenology, Psychology* (Reidel, 1979)
Pinker, S., *The Language Instinct* (William Morrow, 2000)
Pinker S., *Words and Rules* (Weidenfeld and Nicolson, 2000)
Prime, R., *Ramayana* (C and B, 1997)

Reed, J., *Goethe* (Oxford University Press, 1984)
Ridley, M., *Origin of Virtue* (Softback Preview, 1997)
Robinson, D., *Introducing Ethics* (Icon Books, 1998)
Robinson, D., *Lost Languages* (BCA, 2002)
Sarder, Z., *Introducing Culture* (Icon Books, 1997)
Saunders, T., *Plato, The Laws* (Penguin, 1970)
Shand, J., *Philosophy and Philosophers* (Penguin, 1994)
Sprigge, T.L., *Theories of Existence* (Penguin, 1994)
Steiner, G., *Heidegger* (Fontana, 1992)
Tandy, D.W., *Hesoid, Works and Days* (University of California, 1996)
Tarnas, R., *Passions of the Western Mind* (Pimlico, 1991)
Thody, P., *Introducing Barthes* (Icon Books, 1997)
Thody, P., *Introducing Sartre* (Icon Books, 1998)
Thompson, J.A., *Aristotle, Ethics* (Penguin, 1976)
Too, L., *Feng Shui* (Collins and Brown, 1999)
Urmson, J.O., *Western Philosophy and Philosophers* (Routledge, 1989)
Want, C., *Introducing Kant* (Icon Books, 1998)

Mind

Benson, N.C., *Introducing Psychology* (Icon Books, 1997)
Calvin, W., *How Brains Think* (Weidenfeld and Nicolson, 1997)
Carter, R., *Consciousness* (Weidenfeld and Nicolson, 2002)
Carter, R., *Mapping the Mind* (Weidenfeld and Nicolson, 1995)
Damasio, A., *Feeling of What Happens* (Heinemann, 1999)
Dennett, D.C., *Consciousness Explained* (Penguin, 1993)
Dennett, D.C., *Kinds of Minds* (Weidenfeld and Nicolson, 1996)
Diamond, J., *The Evolution of Human Sexuality* (Weidenfeld and Nicolson, 1997)
Evans, D., *Evolutionary Psychology* (Icon Books, 1999)
Ewing, W.A., *Imaging the Human Brain* (Thames and Hudson, 1996)
Furnham, A., *Essence of Psychology* (Whurr, 1990)

Glover, J., *Personal Identity* (Penguin, 1985)
Greenfield, S., *The Human Brain* (Weidenfeld and Nicolson, 1997)
Gregory, R., *The Artful Eye* (Oxford University Press, 1995)
Gregory, R., *The Oxford Companion to Mind* (Oxford University Press, 1987)
Horgan, J., *The Undiscovered Mind* (Weidenfeld and Nicolson, 1995)
Hunt, M., *The Story of Psychology* (Doubleday, 1993)
Hyde, M., *Introducing Jung* (Icon Books, 1997)
Joffe, M., *Jung* (Fontana, 1995)
McMinn, R.M., *Atlas of the Human Anatomy* (Wolfe, 1988)
Mithen, S., *Prehistory of the Mind* (Thames and Hudson, 1996)
Penrose, C., *The Large and the Small of the Human Mind* (Cambridge University Press, 1997)
Pinker, S., *How the Mind Works* (Softback Preview, 1998)
Pinker, S., *The Blank Slate, Denial of Human Nature* (BCA, 2002)
Porter, R., *Cambrige History of Medicine* (Cambridge University Press, 1996)
Ratey, J., *Guide to the Brain* (Little, Brown and Company, 2001)
Searle, J., *Minds, Brains and Science* (Penguin, 1984)
Singer, J., *Hidden Depths of the Soul* (Prism Press, 1994)
Stewart, I., *Figments of Reality* (Cambridge University Press, 1999)
Waterfield, R., *Hypnosis* (Macmillan, 2002)
Webster, R., *Why Freud was Wrong* (HarperCollins, 1998)
Zarato, O., *Introducing Freud* (Icon Books, 1999)